CALLED TO
GREATNESS

*Reflections on vocation and
ambition in the Church*

RAYMOND
TOMKINSON

**kevin
mayhew**

kevin mayhew

First published in Great Britain in 2015 by Kevin Mayhew Ltd
Buxhall, Stowmarket, Suffolk IP14 3BW
Tel: +44 (0) 1449 737978 Fax: +44 (0) 1449 737834
E-mail: info@kevinmayhew.com

www.kevinmayhew.com

9 8 7 6 5 4 3 2 1 0

ISBN 978 1 84867 797 5
Catalogue No. 1501494

Cover design by Rob Mortonson
© Image used under licence from Shutterstock Inc.
Typeset by Angela Selfe

Printed and bound in Great Britain

Contents

Dedication

*For all those who,
in the daily offering of their lives in the service of God,
have been an inspiration to me.*

Acknowledgements

I am grateful to all those who have shared with me their own thoughts, aspirations and experience of ministry in the Church of God. I am deeply grateful, too, to those who have accompanied me on my own ministerial journey and to those who have believed in me and given me opportunities to minister in ways and places beyond my wildest dreams.

I am deeply grateful to my dear wife, Rose. For more than 40 years we have lived out our vocation together, sharing hopes and dreams and many amazing adventures. I am, as always, very grateful to Rose for giving me space to write, knowing that there will be times when I am hopelessly 'lost' in my own thoughts.

Many thanks, too, to those who have encouraged me to write this book, including the Ven. John Cox for his advice and support in the early stages of submission for publication. Thanks are due to the Revd Tom Carson, not only for his encouragement but also for his sterling assistance and advice on both the content and presentation of the manuscript. I am very grateful to Nicki Copeland for her patient editing and to all the team at Kevin Mayhew Limited.

About the author

Raymond Tomkinson spent some time in religious life before becoming a State Registered Nurse specialising in the care of elderly people and in hospice care. He was a hospital manager and staff development officer before training for ordained ministry. He has been a parish priest and area dean in the Church of England and has also held vocations adviser and clergy development posts. He was director of a diocesan retreat centre until 2006. In 2005 he began working at Ripon College Cuddesdon, an Anglican theological college and seminary near Oxford. Following four years serving as a visiting spiritual director he went on to serve for five years as College Chaplain with some teaching responsibilities in the field of Christian spirituality. He continues to be sought out for spiritual direction and to lead quiet days and retreats. Raymond lives in Rutland with his wife, Rose, near their daughter and her family.

Other works by Raymond Tomkinson published by Kevin Mayhew include *Come to me...* (2000), *God's Good Fruit* (2002), *God's Advent People* (2003), *Clothed in Christ* (2008), *Hard Time Praying?* (2009), and *Life Shaping Spirituality* (2014). He is a contributor to *Sermons on Difficult Subjects* (2011) and *Services for Special Occasions* (2012).

Introduction

'In the Christian Church, is ambition a good thing or a bad thing?' This is *not* the question I am asking in this book! I am assuming that ambition is a good thing – but that it needs qualification.

There are other words we might use to avoid using the 'A' word: words such as vision, determination, drive, desire, dreams. As we rehearse these sentiments we may feel a surge of energy, of hope, of expectation. We may begin to ask ourselves how we might make such visions or dreams a reality. Almost certainly, if we feel so inspired, we will want to explore whether or not our vision, our dream, is of God, and we will begin the process of trying to discern the next steps in the fulfilment of that vision or dream.

Hearing the voice of God through others, through the Holy Scriptures or through life-changing events can help us to discern our vocation. Now we can make sense of the energy within us! That sense, intuition, knowledge or experience may cause us to change the way we live, the way we behave or ways in which we use our resources, our gifts and our skills. As we understand our vocation we are energised with ambition to fulfil it. In the inkling of what we might be called to be or to do for God, and in the inkling of what our response to that might be, vocation and ambition come together. They are like two parts of an emulsion which is optimal when shaken together; as the Holy Spirit does the shaking!

What is the alternative to this phenomenon? No inspiration, energy or drive; no vision or dream? If we are honest we might admit that is exactly how it is – sometimes. Another alternative to the life-generating phenomenon of vocation and ambition is fear. It is the fear of being misunderstood or of getting it wrong; of risking everything, losing everything. This may paralyse us into doing nothing, and such paralysis may thwart God's ambition for the world and the role we were to have played in its fulfilment. We may be afraid to embark on anything in case people might think we are doing it for our own satisfaction or to serve our own ego. Again, if we are honest, sometimes that would be exactly what is going on!

The reality, however, is that we are never one hundred per cent altruistic in what we do in the name of God. What might be a 'good thing' to be or to do for God may also give *us* a sense of worth, satisfaction or fulfilment. Might we consider that God wants that for us too? Does not God delight in giving us our heart's desires, especially when our desires are synchronised with God's desires? An endeavour we embark upon may result in bringing us a raised profile in the Church. The platform on which we stand to play our part in the announcement of the kingdom of God may expose us to just a few listening souls or to a vast throng of hearers, some of whom will want to applaud and some of whom will want to run us out of town because what we are about is so challenging, threatening or, in some cultures, illegal. Our vision or dream may change the lives of others for the better, but it may do us no harm either! Conversely, self-serving ambition may completely occlude a God-given vision and the resultant narcissism, corporate or individual, may be destructive, harmful, shameful or scandalous.

Herein lies our greatness: that in spite of the risk that we human beings may subvert God's ambitions into self-aggrandising endeavours he should so enliven us with the presence and power of the Holy Spirit that we *can* be Christ to the world because we belong in Christ. As St Paul puts it, 'and it is no longer I who live, but it is Christ who lives in me. And the life I now live in the flesh I live by faith in the Son of God, who loved me and gave himself for me' (Galatians 2:20).

The aim of this book is to name ambition but not to shame it! It is to explore the relationship between vocation and ambition and to help in the discernment of the difference between laudable ambition and self-serving ambition. The aim is to contribute to debate on the subject and to offer a language for the articulation of God-given ambition that makes the subject less unattractive and demonstrates that laudable ambition is a valuable asset and resource to the Church for the building of the kingdom. Using scriptural and historical references as well as anecdotal evidence of contemporary lived experience, I aim to demonstrate that ambition has always been part of Christian life in both its reasonably altruistic and its egocentric manifestations.

In the opening chapter I address the 'A' word full on. I acknowledge that it is used warily in the culture of the Church and I hasten to qualify what I mean by it: simply the distinction between laudable ambition and self-serving ambition. We recognise, too, that it is sometimes difficult to distinguish one from the other, especially when the word is not used openly.

In an atmosphere of confidence and trust, people will speak to me of their ambitions. Some might appear to be self-serving, but when they are explored further it often becomes evident that the furtherance of God's kingdom is at the heart of them. Energy and zeal become tangible as aspirations and visions are shared and described. In humility and simplicity, those who have offered themselves in the service of God reveal the depth of their love for God and for their neighbour. They reveal their need for a broad 'canvas' on which to paint their visions, their need for scope to make a difference in the world around them.

In this first chapter I introduce the reader to four characters who have met up at a conference. They are quite different from one another and have widely differing lay or ordained ministries. They crop up again in later chapters to help us to explore aspects of vocation, ambition and the outworking of them in Christian ministry.

In the next chapter we reflect more fully on what we understand vocation to mean. We recognise that the word 'vocation' has gone through some changes of use and meaning, that in recent centuries it has been associated with clergy or vowed religious and that in more recent times it has become associated with certain professional vocational pathways. Here we acknowledge and lament that the Church has the ongoing task of reacquainting the people of God with the truth that we all have a calling.

In the third chapter we reflect on what we understand God's ambitions to be. Under the overarching theme of God's ambitious love, I discuss this subject under three main Trinitarian headings: God's creative and re-creative ambition; God's redemptive, restorative and relational ambition; and God the Holy Spirit's declared ambition to 'renew the face of the earth' (Psalm 104:30, NLT). Our consideration of God's ambition will be determined, to a greater or lesser extent, by what we believe about God. We compare our own credo with our understanding of what God wants for all creation.

With the help of biblical scholarship we explore what we believe we know about God, recognising both the centrality of the revelation of God in Jesus Christ and the danger of circumscribing God, of making God too small and too knowable. Reflection on what we believe God's ambitions to be is key to reflecting on how we, as God's people, are to respond, to 'lean in' to God's purposes. We marvel that God wants us to cooperate and to collaborate with him in the fulfilment of his ambitions and recognise that this is part of our call to greatness; not that we are great but that God is great and our identity in Christ brings us both the privilege of greatness and the responsibility to live out that greatness in humble servanthood. Here we begin to reflect on the nature of the kingdom of God.

This chapter includes a reflection on the account in St John's Gospel of the marriage feast in Cana which, I believe, illustrates well the generosity and love of God in creative, redemptive and salvation terms and the way that God coming to earth in humankind tells us that God's kingdom is like no other!

In the fourth chapter we reflect on the Church's response to God's missional and kingdom ambitions. God's vision for the kingdom is ambitious, and the role of the universal Church is thought to be crucial to the fulfilment of it. But I pose the question, 'If there is no agreed vision of it, can there be a concerted effort to bring it about?' I argue that while there is dispute about the *nature* of the kingdom, there is more scope for individual and human ambition to reign.

I encourage the reader to ask how easy or how difficult it is to link what we do, how we live, our church life and focus, or what we spend, with what we believe about the kingdom of God. How often do we ask, 'What has this endeavour, expenditure, initiative, got to do with announcing or forwarding the kingdom of God?' I assert that the position a church community takes on the ambitions of God in terms of the kingdom should determine its local policy and drive its fund-raising and expenditure. So a key question here is, 'Who has the voice of authority in determining what is the best policy for leaning into God's ambition?'

We are familiar with the way that Holy Scripture is used (and abused) in order to promote a particular stance on almost any matter. In the same way, the earnest direction of an individual, or a group of individuals, can steamroll a church congregation or community into believing that the kingdom of God is characterised in such-and-such a way without consultation, discussion or consensus, in a way that the early Church would not recognise. Through organisational and institutional bullying, human and material resources can be diverted to the fulfilment of self-serving ambition.

In this chapter, too, we reflect on Christ's commission:

'Go therefore and make disciples of all nations, baptizing them in the name of the Father and of the Son and of the Holy Spirit, and teaching them to obey everything that I have commanded you. And remember, I am with you always, to the end of the age.'

Matthew 28:19, 20

These words of Christ are sometimes called 'The Great Commission'. With these words, Christ calls his disciples to witness to the gospel to the ends of the earth. This was their commissioning, and it is ours too.

Jesus taught us that: 'the kingdom of God is among you' (Luke 17:21), but we, the Church, '. . . have this treasure in clay jars, so that it may be made clear that this extraordinary power belongs to God and does not come from us' (2 Corinthians 4:7). In chapter five, therefore, we come to the fulfilment of God's ambition (whatever we decide that is!) through fragile human beings. Beginning with a reflection on words attributed to St Teresa of Avila, we ponder on the premise that Christ has no body but ours; no hands, no feet on earth but ours. Here we acknowledge and celebrate that both greatness and smallness are true Christian characteristics because God has planted the greatness of himself deep inside us, and the awesomeness of that reality moves us to adopt a disposition of smallness.

In the history of the Christian Church there have been countless 'witnesses' – ordinary human beings who have lived extraordinary lives in the service of God: people who are both great and small. In this chapter we consider a few of them, in particular two biblical characters: Mary the mother of Jesus, and John the Baptist.

As we consider our human frailty, we reflect on the paradox of the conflict within us that leads us to do the things we should do and also to do the things we should *not* do. We explore further the relationship between altruism and self-centredness: how we live on a sliding scale between two extremes and how God uses even our less-than-altruistic traits to further his purposes.

At its best, our self-interest is the need for appreciation, recognition and sincere praise. We consider how, in some secular organisations, this is regarded not as patronisation but as a matter of meeting human need for appreciation, satisfaction and fulfilment, while acknowledging that it can also be about enhancing employees' response to meeting the aims and objectives of the organisation. Above all, we reflect on how we are commissioned in the service of God in our woundedness. We consider the post-resurrection Christ with outstretched hands that still bear the wounds of crucifixion.

Keeping in mind the potential 'slide' away from altruism in the direction of self-centredness, in chapter six we begin to explore what happens when we are tempted to misuse power. Our reflections in this chapter are based on the scriptural accounts of the temptations faced by Jesus in the desert following his baptism by John. We consider this in terms of the power to change things; the temptation to 'glory' in adulation, celebrity and fame; and the myth of invincibility fuelled by a lack of self-knowledge or of self-awareness. This leads to a discussion about the paradox of power and powerlessness; power and vulnerability, which come together in the mystery of the cross.

In chapter seven we reflect on what happens when there is a further movement away from altruism and towards self-centredness and self-absorption. Set in the context of discussion about the impact on the Church's ministry of individuals in positions of leadership or influence and how personality type, personal style and motivation can shape the Church for better or for worse, we consider narcissism, which is common to us all (to some degree), but which becomes more serious when it is a personality disorder. Narcissism, as a serious disorder, is a common problem in the Church and comes in many forms. Some of these are not easy to recognise and we explore, a little, possible root causes of it. If, like me, the reader is not a psychologist or sociologist but merely an observer of human behaviour, you may welcome the findings of trained researchers and practitioners in those disciplines. So, in this chapter, in order to aid our reflections, I have called upon the work of a couple of experts and their published opinions.

In the last chapter we reflect, just a little, on what might help to steer us closer to living more faithfully and authentically our Christian vocation. We reflect on a number of themes and issues raised in previous chapters. We consider the potential positive impact upon the Church of more honesty, openness and celebration of those whom God is calling to be leaders among us and how this might help to identify potentially serious narcissism before it is too late.

We consider the liberating power of being content with what we have been called to be and to do. We explore what we might understand to be governance in the Church and how this, too, might enable us to contain seriously damaging self-serving ambition through being realistic about ourselves: about our potential and limitations.

We explore what the Rule of St Benedict has to offer in the governance of our community and congregational life, in particular with regard to listening to one another. The Rule of St Benedict is full of love, compassion and common sense, and has stood the test of time as a good model for living a Christ-centred life – a life worthy of our calling to greatness. It is offered as one model of servanthood in leadership, the leader being 'shepherd', 'healer' and 'doctor'.

This book is based in my own 'worldview' and in that of women and men, both ordained and lay, who have shared with me their views, dreams, joys, inspirations, experiences, dilemmas, heartaches, hurts and disappointments. I have also drawn inspiration from relevant authorities in related fields and disciplines, offering direct quotations where they may aid the reader's reflection. I have tried to keep these to a minimum.

In order to illustrate some of the reflections on vocation and ambition I have created scenarios based on factual events. However, I have used fictional characters to tell the stories, thus protecting the identity of those whose experiences have contributed to this book.

Sprinkled throughout the book are opportunities to **Pause for reflection.** My hope is that they may be helpful either for personal reflection or as an aid to group discussion.

I do not believe God should be regarded as being gender-specific, but rather than resort to less familiar and somewhat contrived and cumbersome expressions such as 'God's-self' or the like I have stayed with the convention of God as 'he' or 'him' and pray that 'she' and the reader will understand.

CHAPTER ONE

Greatness and ambition: named but not shamed

The Conference Four: a story of greatness and of ambition

Derek, Christine, Hugo and Ruth bumped into one another over coffee in the lobby of the vast conference centre. The occasion was a diocesan conference entitled 'Going for God'. The attendees, clerical and lay people all in strategic posts around the diocese, had just eaten a delicious dinner supplemented by a generous provision of wine (a gift from the bishop). The mood was vibrant, the conversation animated and the noise almost unbearable! Ruth, Derek, Christine and Hugo rarely saw one another except on such occasions. Christine, a deanery lay chairperson, had known Derek a long time but previously knew Hugo and Ruth only by sight.

Following a day of intense discussions, Derek was not in the mood for conversation, so he wandered in the direction of the 'graffiti wall' – a place for attendees to make comments throughout the day. There he saw Ruth and Christine. Ruth was writing a pithy response to a comment that had been made by another, which she regarded as inappropriate. She signed her own comment and underlined her signature.

'Is that wise?' asked Derek with a glint in his eye.

'I have nothing to lose!' remarked Ruth with wry humour. Christine smiled but said nothing.

Hugo spotted Derek and Ruth, sped across the room to them and, without greeting them, announced, 'I've spoken to three bishops, two archdeacons and the Dean today! It's important to be seen, you know.'

Hugo had always thought it important to raise his profile. He was a skilled lobbyist and had a charm that made him a little less irritating than he might otherwise have been. In his current parish ministry Hugo had fought for, and achieved, a new church school and had reordered the interior of the parish church. This was an imaginative project which brought both flexibility to the worship space and excellent concert facilities which capitalised on the good acoustics of the building. By anyone's estimation, Hugo's ministry had been fruitful. However, in recent years he had begun to take less and less notice of the opinion of the people around him, and some of his more recent schemes and projects had caused distress to some of his parishioners and concern to the diocese.

Somewhat as an afterthought, Hugo introduced himself to Christine. On hearing that she was a deanery lay chairperson he sought connections between them: people they might know in common. Sensing that further conversation with Christine would avail him little, he turned back to the other two with the words, 'Must dash. I'm heading up a ginger group in the small meetings room.'

As Hugo parted from the company he asked, 'Why have I not got on?' He didn't wait for an answer, which was fortunate because none of the other three had an answer for him.

As he returned to studying the graffiti wall, Derek muttered a question of his own: 'What does "getting on" look like?'

Ruth replied, 'Don't ask me; I will never know.'

'Quite,' responded Christine. Their wry smiles turned to brief laughter before they continued to sip their coffee thoughtfully.

Ruth's ordained ministry had begun at a time when women priests in the Church of England were just beginning to find their feet. What had seemed impossible, or at least unlikely, just a few years before was now a reality, but what kind of reality was it in those early days? The Church then was (and still is) ambivalent about women's ministry. In some circles Ruth was welcomed and her ministry embraced. In others she was shunned: women and men, clergy and lay, would leave the building if she exercised her priestly orders. Ruth always suspected that she had been selected for ministry because it was thought she would be compliant, that she wouldn't make waves and would be no threat to male colleagues seeking to 'get on': priests like Hugo rather than priests like Derek.

The Church had completely underestimated Ruth's spirit as well as her abilities. After serving her title under a male incumbent, she had been encouraged to consider a chaplaincy role, perhaps in a hospital. Perhaps she might consider part-time work: after all, as a wife and mother, surely she must want to give priority to her family? With her pastoral, organisational and leadership gifts and skills, together with a sound academic background and a flair for teaching, Ruth felt called to take a fuller role in the life of the Church.

To stand her ground for the ministry to which she felt called had been costly for Ruth, and for her family, whose support she had always enjoyed. For as many as would be inclined to keep her out of the way there were as many encouraging her: en-couraging her; making her courageous. She found that the ceiling (even the infamous glass ceiling) did not fall in if she spoke out and stuck up for what she believed was right. Ruth became well known in the diocese and was loved and admired by many. Some of those with theological and ecclesiological objections to her ministry continued to treat her coolly, though not with the degree of hostility she had experienced at the beginning of her ministry.

Ruth, now an area dean and a much-valued member of several diocesan committees, had found a degree of fulfilment, but she recognised that prejudice against women in ministry was so ingrained in the Church that it would impact upon her for the remainder of her ministry and beyond. Her remark to Derek, 'What have I got to lose?' was not a whimper of hopelessness, self-pity or despair; a giving-up on any future possibilities, so much as a cry of strength and triumph. Ruth had found that boldness, fearlessness and the discovery of her own worth meant that she could stand tall before her God and his Church as a testament to faithfulness, commitment and the value of painful sacrifice.

Derek's equally long ministry had been unremarkable. He had stayed in parish ministry serving in two different parts of the diocese. He had steered his flock through the many ministerial, ecclesial, pastoral and liturgical changes that characterised the Church in the late twentieth and early twenty-first centuries.

Christine could not remember when church was not part of her life. For most of her life she had lived in a village where the local church and its activities were central to relationships and neighbourliness. Christine had, in her time, undertaken most jobs in and around the village church: everything from cleaning the brass to being churchwarden. She understood her duty to God and to her neighbour. She was much loved for her quiet wisdom and her deep pastoral care which was demonstrated in generosity of spirit and absolute discretion. People would never know all that she had done for so many people.

Christine's local vicar had encouraged her to participate in the activities of the local deanery, and latterly she had been persuaded to take on the role of deanery lay chairperson. She didn't enjoy getting involved in the politics of the Church and could be quite dismayed by the behaviour of some of the local clergy, but she was always gracious and generous. Christine could be very gentle in the delivery of hard truths and was not to be underestimated in either her abilities or her strength of character. Her quiet encouragement of the ministry of others had had a profoundly positive effect on the life of the deanery. Greatness in humility characterised her reputation.

Christine, Hugo, Ruth and Derek. We may ask ourselves which of these four people are called to greatness, which are ambitious. I suggest the answer is that they are all called to greatness and that they are all ambitious. They are all ambitious for the things of God. They each draw their inspiration from what they understand God's ambition to be, what they understand the kingdom of God to be like. All four have offered themselves for ministry with the heartfelt desire to make a difference in the Church and in the world. All have offered their gifts, their energy and their zeal. All have sought and found some personal satisfaction in the course of their ministry. None of them are completely altruistic but all seek to live authentically and truthfully before the God they know and love. God does not require complete altruism, but truth: an honest understanding of complex humanity employed in the service of God.

Their call to greatness rests in the great God who called them into life: called them into new and everlasting life by their baptism into Christ. From that moment on they have had the dignity and greatness of being members of the household of faith, part of the royal priesthood, princes and princesses in the kingdom of God. Their call to greatness and their adoption would instil in them a deep sense of gratitude and a desire to make God's love, mercy and grace known to the world (at least to the world in which they live and move and have their being). Making Christ known is their first and greatest ambition. Hearing about and learning about God's ambition for the world has continued to inspire each of the faithful four to serve God in ministries within the Church as they offer their personality traits, their gifts, their time, their energy and their zeal in the service of God.

Some rather more entrepreneurial readers might think that the achievements of the four are too modest, that more could have been expected of them. It may be tempting to ask where it all went wrong. We might want to say of Hugo that the time he spent lobbying the 'great and the good' might have been better spent visiting the sick. We might want to suggest that a little more guidance and accountability, as well as a little more training in communicating his ideas to people, might have prevented some of his more ambitious projects from causing alarm. We might want to say of Ruth that prejudice, lack of courage or imagination has prevented her from exercising an episcopal ministry so far. Possibly. We might want to say that Derek's lifetime of reassuring his flock has prevented him and them from taking risks, has held them all back from moving on, and so leaves his ministerial successor an enormous task. We might want to say of Christine that quiet parochial neighbourliness has not significantly increased the numbers of people seated on the pews of the village church.

How does one measure the value of the contribution each one of us makes? Ruth, Christine, Derek and Hugo have all, to some extent, fulfilled their ambitions – both their personal ones and their God-inspired ones. Each has followed their inspirational lights and each has made a difference. Perhaps that is all any of us can ask!

The stories of Christine, Hugo, Ruth and Derek may raise other questions. We will return to their stories, and hear those of others, hoping that they may help us to identify some of the questions that need addressing in the Church and give us pause for thought about our own discipleship and ministry. We will consider further what it means, as Christians, to be called to greatness, but first we need to confront the subject of ambition in the Church.

Using the 'A' word

The library at Ripon College Cuddesdon[1] has more than 30,000 books. The catalogue indicates that there is only one book with a title that includes the word 'ambition'. It is the autobiography of James T. M. Pong, a twentieth-century bishop of Taiwan, and the book was published for private circulation. Even then, the title implies a pejorative perspective – *Worldly Ambition Versus Christian Vocation* – and points to the apparent irreconcilability of the phenomenon of ambition and the Christian ethic.

Perhaps the Bible can enlighten us. Again, the word is found only in certain translations and then only in relation to self-serving ambition. Yet God's ambition for the world and the ambition of servants such as St Paul is well evidenced. One such reference uses the word with qualification. We hear, for instance, Paul teasing out the difference between laudable or worthy ambition and selfish ambition:

> Some proclaim Christ from envy and rivalry, but others from goodwill. These proclaim Christ out of love, knowing that I have been put here for the defence of the gospel; the others proclaim Christ out of selfish ambition, not sincerely but intending to increase my suffering in my imprisonment.
>
> *Philippians 1:15-17*

---

[1] An Anglican theological college, seminary and study centre near Oxford, England.

Paul sounds as though he has suffered as a result of the selfish ambitions of fellow Christians. He teaches that to authentically proclaim Christ by both word and deed, our motive for doing so has to be rooted in Christ-like love.

The absence of the word 'ambition' in books hints at the problem upon which we shall reflect. First, however, we explore what *we* might mean by 'ambition' and consider whether or not it has a rightful place in the life of the Church. We ask ourselves, too, if there is a legitimate place for related phenomena such as recognition, appreciation and personal profile. We may want to conclude that such things shine the spotlight on the servants of God rather than on the God being served and that they are not to be encouraged. We may be more comfortable with attributes such as vision, boldness, daring, courage, drive and initiative. Stories abound of Christians in every generation who have done great things for God and his kingdom and who have not courted recognition, appreciation or personal profile. Sometimes we have acclaimed them and continue to celebrate their achievements long after they are dead. On the other hand, we may believe that they have their reward in heaven and that nothing is to be gained by recalling or celebrating achievements made when they were alive perhaps many centuries ago.

There are those, too, whose discipleship is celebrated while they are still alive! They are held up to us as exemplars. Whether or not they like it, they acquire a 'following'. Do we find that heart-warming or do we find that idea obnoxious? Are such people ambitious? Would they ever declare their ambitions out loud?

Stories of ambition

It has been a privilege to engage with those in training for ordained ministry. I hear of their ambitions, though they rarely use the word. Interestingly, a visiting preacher to the seminary (himself a retired and very senior churchman) began his sermon by wondering what might be the ambition of the ordinands seated before him. He wondered if they had an ambition to be a good pastor or a good preacher or teacher. The preacher did not affirm such ambitions but dismissed them since, he argued, God would make of them what he wished.

Some ordinands were rather disappointed with the preacher's dismissal of what they regarded as wholesome ambition. What would be wrong with wanting to be a good preacher, teacher or pastor? The best defence I could come up with was that there was an implication in the sermon that God can do great things through us whether or not we turn out to be good at this or that aspect of ministry. However, the New Testament Church learned to recognise gifts and the ministries that derive from them:

> And God has appointed in the church first apostles, second prophets, third teachers; then deeds of power, then gifts of healing, forms of assistance, forms of leadership, various kinds of tongues. Are all apostles? Are all prophets? Are all teachers? Do all work miracles? Do all possess gifts of healing? Do all speak in tongues? Do all interpret? But strive for the greater gifts. And I will show you a still more excellent way.
>
> *1 Corinthians 12:28-31*

There is liberation to be found in recognising what is *not* one's gift. It helps us to overcome the hardening of the 'oughteries' that can be so disabling. There can be a degree of relief or liberation in letting go of self-delusion, and the exercise of letting go is thought to be one which nurtures the virtue of humility. In the life of the Church, this exercise in spiritual growth is not matched by its corollary: the recognition, in honesty and truth, that one *is* gifted in a certain way. Affirmation of our gifts is so often thwarted by self-doubt or by our belief that those who would affirm our gifts are biased because they love us.

The problem of under-affirmation is a stain which goes deep into the fabric of Church life. Sincere praise does not always come readily to the lips of those who have a care for gifts and ministries. There would seem to be a view that affirmation will lead to pride and the absence of affirmation will lead to humility. According to Desiderius Erasmus, humility is truth. St Vincent de Paul said something similar. He held that humility is truth and that pride is nothing but a lie. Are we being truthful when we decline to affirm others in their gifts in order to keep them humble? Are our motives for declining to affirm gifts in others that are clearly God-given ever totally altruistic? I think not, but we may summon up enough generosity of spirit to overcome our less than worthy pride or vanity.

Your Church needs ambitious you!

There is encouragement to be found in accounts of how the Church is trying to recruit those with the gifts it needs to fulfil its purpose of building the kingdom of God. In recent times, for example, the Church has recognised that it is going to need more theological educators as the Church grasps more fully the implication of its mission and ministry through all its members, women and men, lay and ordained, who will need to be equipped for such mission. In identifying the gifts it needs in those who offer themselves for ministry, it would be good if such people could be let in on the secret.

Sometimes hints are dropped in the ear during the discernment process or during training, but rarely do such people hear unequivocally that they have been selected because it is generally agreed that they are likely to deliver an educative, senior leadership or episcopal role within the Church. Indeed, at selection conferences for ordained ministry in the Church of England, reports indicate whether someone is a 'potential theological educator'.

Those offering themselves for ordained ministry will speak openly about a sense of call to priestly orders, but would not dare to admit to a sense of call to the episcopate! Occasionally, in a very safe conversation, and with encouragement, an ordinand will admit to a sense of a call to the episcopate or some other 'senior' role in the life of the Church. Such women and men, in my experience, are not self serving, vain or puffed up with pride. Quite the reverse! Their aspirations lie in vision and zeal for the building of the kingdom of God. Although they are ready and willing to serve their time in formational roles, they already sense the need for a broader canvas on which to paint. Some have come from secular employment where such ambition was praised and encouraged, where their potential as leaders was spotted at an interview for a relatively junior post. Such gifting and such potential is not left behind when they respond to the call to ordained ministry. God calls them as they are. So often we may say, by way of consolation, that God has called us not in spite of our weaknesses and our failings but because of them. So seldom would we say that God has called us because of our ambition or our self-knowing, honest appraisal of our gifts and talents.

God's humble, human, ambitious servants

There is a lot of talk about servanthood in ministry, but clergy are put into a benefice to lead: to lead like a shepherd leads; not to lord it over their congregations but certainly to exercise authority on behalf of the people of God. How exactly that servanthood is to be exercised is the stuff of many lectures in ministerial training and much debate in the life of the Church. It would seem that humility and appropriate ambition is a balance that is difficult to strike and to sustain. There is a real need here to check that humility is real and not false; that it is not a cover for cowardice or an attempt to draw sympathy when censure would be more appropriate.

Zeal for your house has consumed me!

Is not 'zeal', which is at the heart of much of Christian ministry, another word for ambition? Zeal gets us out of bed in the morning! For example, it is zeal that drives clergy to work so hard to make Christmas services so special, so evocative or innovative in an attempt to draw people closer to the Christ-child. Yet at a January clergy chapter meeting, the conversation may sound more like rivalry than zeal as clergy compare notes on church attendance: 'We had 150 at the Midnight.' 'We had 300 and they were standing in the aisles.' 'We had 400 and had to relay the service outside!'

Is zeal diminished by such rivalry? I think not. Beneath and behind it is ambition which is never totally altruistic but which has, for the most part, sufficient selfless purpose in it to make a God-given difference in the world.

God's competitive servants

There are physical monuments to self-serving endeavours based in rivalry and competition. In a rural setting in East

Anglia is a memorial garden. It hasn't been there very long. It came about following consultation in the village about what to do with a piece of land on which had stood an Anglican Church which had been built there in the nineteenth century but which had needed to be demolished in recent years because it was sinking into the ground and had become unsafe to use. The church had been built in the Gothic style and of sizeable proportions, its two heavy gable ends being the cause of its eventual breaking up.

The church had been built as a 'daughter church' from a neighbouring parish because there were two Methodist chapels in the village but no Anglican one. The village had never had a large population and so it would always be a struggle to maintain three buildings. Moreover, worshipping villagers were split into three groups rather than two. Subsequently both Methodist chapels closed, and when the Anglican church became unsafe the congregation began to worship in the only other public building in the village: the village hall. By this time those of Methodist or Anglican heritage were worshipping together.

Following the move to the village hall, the size of the congregation increased, and it continues to flourish. Meanwhile the site of what was once the Anglican church is a place in which to reflect. Here, we reflect on how rivalry split a worshipping community into three groups for more than 150 years, but how God and nature have brought the remnant of worshipping Christians together in joint witness and outreach.

We might say that this was a case of an ambitious building underpinned (evidently inadequately!) not by altruism but by rivalry and competition. There is, of course, good ambition, ambition to build the kingdom of God, which is surely the one agreed ambition of the universal Church? But when it comes to how that kingdom is to be announced and advanced, this pure and holy ambition may be subverted by human ambition that is more about building our own empires, our own kingdoms. Ambition in the Church ranges from the 'mega-vicar' who would be Archbishop of Canterbury by the age of 26 to the congregant who would be churchwarden so that they can stop all that nonsense about putting in a toilet or taking out the pews. A glance through the Church press (not to mention the popular secular press) renders enough evidence to convict us all!

If we checked out every debate or argument in Church life with the question, 'Whose kingdom is being built here?' we might make some rather different decisions. Unfortunately, however, we are unlikely ever all to agree on what the kingdom of God should look like in spite of the teaching of Jesus and of the apostles.

Jesus did not say that there would not be the greatest among his disciples; only that the greatest should consider themselves the least (Luke 22:24-27). Does this introduce a competitive element to kingdom building? Only by revisiting the words of Jesus, only by reflecting upon them together, can we begin to model our Church life according to Christ's precepts. But where do we start? What Scripture can be a springboard for changing something so ingrained in Church life as self-serving competitiveness?

The story of the two sons of Zebedee and their mother's request in Matthew's Gospel may offer us a focus for reflection (Matthew 20:20-23). Jesus is already aware that the mother of James and John is ambitious for her sons. Jesus has just painted a picture of the kingdom but in her mind's eye, and in that of her sons and of others, there is glory and honour and power to be had and she wants some of that for her boys. Jesus, knowing the answer already, asks, 'What do you want?' He asks if James and John can pay the price that he will pay: the sacrifice of his own life. That wasn't quite what Mum had intended for her boys! The sad irony is that both James and John would become great apostles and would do great things for the kingdom, but Mum would lose both her boys to a martyr's death.

Pause for reflection

You may like to stop reading at this point and, for a few moments, place yourself in the scene, among the gathered disciples. Eavesdrop on the exchanges between Jesus and the other characters. Reflect a little on what greatness and being the servant of all means. When you are ready, may I ask you to imagine Jesus turning his gaze from James and John and looking directly at you? You hear Jesus ask you, 'What do you want?' In the silence of your heart, consider your reply.

Advice from the apostles

Perhaps the advice of Paul will help: 'Do nothing from selfish ambition or conceit, but in humility regard others as better than yourselves. Let each of you look not to your own interests, but to the interests of others' (Philippians 2:3, 4). These words follow that great passage about humbling oneself. Paul is acutely aware that, sometimes, competitiveness is unhealthy and is rooted in the selfish ambitions of party-men seeking to outdo or outwit him. However, in his letter to the Galatians, Paul betrays his own competitive streak when he writes, 'I advanced in Judaism beyond many among my people of the same age, for I was far more zealous for the traditions of my ancestors' (Galatians 1:14).

The advice of the apostle James may speak to us:

> But if you have bitter envy and selfish ambition in your
> hearts, do not be boastful and false to the truth. Such
> wisdom does not come down from above, but is earthly,
> unspiritual, devilish. For where there is envy and selfish
> ambition, there will also be disorder and wickedness of
> every kind. But the wisdom from above is first pure, then
> peaceable, gentle, willing to yield, full of mercy and good
> fruits, without trace of partiality or hypocrisy. And a
> harvest of righteousness is sown in peace for those who
> make peace.
>
> *James 3:14-18*

The connotation here is of a whole raft of unacceptable (even
sinful?) behaviour surrounding selfish ambition. We read here
of rivalry, competitiveness and even attempts to increase the
suffering of others. Yet, could we always claim competitiveness
and rivalry to be a bad thing? Elsewhere St Paul asks, 'Do
you not know that in a race the runners all compete, but
only one receives the prize? Run in such a way that you may
win it' (1 Corinthians 9:24). Who else is in the race, bearing
in mind that the goal must be the same, the prize open to
all? The race would appear to be more than a competition
against the enemies of Christ's Church – it is rather a matter
of outdoing one another in zeal. We may remember that Paul
was a zealous person even before his conversion. He was very
energetic at what he did to persecute Christians. Following
his conversion Paul was no less zealous a person than he had
been before, only now he was zealous for the gospel of Jesus
Christ (Philippians 3:6).

How does our zeal, our competitiveness and our desire to
outdo each other in doing good, appear to those beyond the

Church? The non-Christian with worldly ambition picking up the Church press or reported news from the General Synod might easily recognise their own cut-and-thrust world of argument, debate, backbiting and ruthless ambition. They might ask, 'What's the problem?'

We might respond, 'Well, you see, the Church is not supposed to be like this.' And we show them the words of Jesus:

Blessed are the meek, for they will inherit the earth.
Matthew 5:5
The greatest among you will be your servant.
Matthew 23:11

Those who find their life will lose it, and those who lose their life for my sake will find it.
Matthew 10:39

At this point a non-Christian at the top of their ambitious game may justly respond, 'But that's not how your Church is!' The gap between the way the Church is and its aspirational hope is viewed through the lens of its understanding of its vocation.

In the next two chapters we explore the subject of vocation in more depth before we go on to consider God's ambition for the world.

CHAPTER TWO

Vocation and ambition

How do we use the term 'vocation'?

The word 'vocation' has gone through some changes of use and meaning. Much has depended on what people have believed to be the nature of 'call' and whether or not that call is something special – rare, even – and is associated with certain occupations or certain kinds of endeavour and whether it is associated with specially gifted or saintly people. Moreover, we might be drawn to understand vocation as a call by God to an individual and not to the whole Church or to all God's people on earth. If we corral vocation as being relevant only to people of particular gifting or occupation, we are left with the problem of what we understand to be the God-givenness, value or dignity of the rest of the people in the world. Demarcation between the vocational and the rest so often brings with it a differential value: the vocational being held in awe and the non-vocational being redacted and understood as of lesser value. The term 'vocation' is sometimes applied to occupations that are professionally accredited and to endeavours which seem more obviously to make a positive difference to the quality of people's lives. Among such vocational pathways we might cite doctors, nurses, teachers and lawyers.

The dilemma is further compounded when people within supposedly vocational occupations hold differing views on whether or not their role or occupation is indeed vocational. If we were to ask a group of teachers or nurses if they understand their occupation as vocational, we are likely to discover that some think it is while others consider it to be just a job. Much will depend on what they understand 'vocation' to mean. To them it might be a word which dignifies their occupation above that of other work. It will depend, too, on whether they feel called by society to undertake such work or whether they believe in God and understand their work as a response to God's invitation or command. Even then, they may hold that God calls people to a particular function or, on the other hand, that God leaves people to do what they think best!

The reader will notice that I have not yet mentioned clergy! Those in our church whose ministry is to help people to discover and to respond appropriately to their vocation have their work cut out in promoting vocation as both a call to the whole Church and a call to all individuals, in a culture which has, for centuries, confined the concept to clergy and vowed religious. For at least 100 years, clergy have been suffering from an identity crisis! Well-documented and discussed debates continue in high or central places within Church denominations and locally within congregations.

Essentially, our purpose on earth, whether we are ordained or lay, is written in the Scriptures. Jesus, in his summary of the law, brings a sublime and awesome imprimatur to this revelation: giving love the status of law (Mark 12:30-31; see also Luke 10:27). What we are *for* is to love and to serve God: to participate in God's life and purpose, and to share in God's initiative in bringing in his kingdom of love. We have Christ's commandment to love one another (John 15:17), but how can God legislate for our loving response? Surely love has to be freely given. But in his command to 'love one another' (John 13:34, 35), Jesus reminds us that it is not enough to love God: love must be expressed, lived out in love for others, with Jesus' own example of love before us. For John, living in love and living in God are synonymous. 'God is love, and those who abide in love abide in God, and God abides in them' (1 John 4:16b). If we are to follow this teaching we must recognise that *all* our living is bound up with God's love and our loving response. The love of God *for* us calls for a response *from* us. We have been gifted and graced by a loving God who wants us to make the most of what we have been given. God wants us to deploy all that we are and all that we do in ways which honour him and which express our love for him and for our neighbour. In this sense all that is born of love in us is to shape our life and service. Our vocation is born of love and is to serve lovingly. It is this same love that energises us. Discerning how love can be best expressed in our ministry can take time and needs reviewing regularly because we grow, we change and life around us changes and affects what we can offer and what can be received from us.

George's story

George became a priest after a career as a butler. In his last post before training for the ministry he worked in a large country house which in former days had a large indoor and outdoor staff but in recent years had been run by a small team. To ensure the smooth running of the house, for the benefit of the resident family and for the tourists who were allowed access to the house a few days each week, members of staff had to be prepared to undertake tasks that were not strictly part of their remit. George not only took care of the cellar and had oversight of the household budget, but he also learned to turn his hand to anything from polishing the hall floor to arranging flowers in the drawing room.

Once ordained, George served as a curate in a suburban church and, characteristically, threw himself into any activity he could. In his first autumn in the parish he found himself helping members of the congregation with preparations for the harvest festival celebration. While busy arranging orange, gold and red flowers on a large pedestal in the church porch, George was startled by a voice behind him saying, 'George, you've missed your vocation!'

George laughed off the comment but it stuck in his mind. It was just one of those things people say. It was said as a compliment, so why did he feel bruised by it?

No matter how sure we might be that we are doing what God wants us to be doing, we can all wonder if we heard our call correctly. Should we have stayed on another path? Is this path right for now but might the direction change? How often we find that what we are doing now calls upon so much of what we have done in the past! In the economy of God, nothing we have ever done or experienced is wasted – not even the things we did that were contrary to God's law. Even they can be transfigured into something of value. Sadly, one hears so often that those steering or guiding people along an ordained ministerial vocational pathway leave the ordinands with the impression that nothing they did before ordination has any relevance to the ministry ahead of them!

We might reflect, too, on whether or not we consider what we do between one Sunday worship and the next as being part and parcel of our God-given vocation and our participation in God's ambition for the world. Do our local church leaders even know what we do during the week? Do they affirm our vocation in what we do?

We might want to ask how arranging flowers in the church porch helps to proclaim or bring in the kingdom of God. Well, we could consider the welcome they offer to the stranger: the delight their beauty might bring. We could consider the way George was not too proud to work with his skilled hands in the service of the church community and how that might encourage others to offer their own God-given talents in the service of God and his Church. In the service of the vocation of the whole Church, this modest occupation needs no further dignification or qualification, but there is more to George's vocation than flower arranging. If someone were to thank us regularly for a particular gift we exercise we might feel affirmed in that gift, but we might also want to respond by declaring that there is more to me than that! This was a significant part of George's discombobulation.

Pause for reflection

Do you have a talent or skill you offer in the service of others which you do not recognise as being vocational: the application of what you have to offer in the service of God and his people? Do you think it too commonplace or trivial to be given the status of vocation?

So, what *do* we mean by the term 'vocation'?

The Greek words καλέω (to call, summon forth) and κλῆσις (calling, vocation) are used prolifically in the New Testament and are implicit in many other texts. For example, Jesus *calls* us to repentance. He *calls* fishermen to follow him. Our primary task is not some work or activity taken on in the name of God. First and foremost our *call* is to God. It is a call to holiness, to faithfulness. It is a call to worship and to adore God. This is what we are for! It is, of course, a *response* to God's call: the God who called us into life and into new life in Jesus Christ.

In order to take a closer look at what we mean by vocation, it might be useful to divide the subject into categories, or dimensions. Perhaps we could think of it as being rather like a valuable diamond which sparkles gloriously because it has been cut and shaped with many facets to reflect the light. So it is with vocation. It may help to think of the facets of vocation as taking us from the broadest possible understanding of it, such as our vocation to belong to the human race, to the very particular of it – what we might call our personal vocation.

We call to mind the Reverend George arranging flowers in the church porch. He knows he has a vocation to be a member of the human race. He is a human being before ever he is a human 'doing'! He is not identified by what he does – or is he? As we noted in the introduction to this chapter, so often our vocational identity is spoken of, or thought of, in terms of what we *do*, and the seeming 'worthiness' of what we do is given its own hierarchical status.

George recognises, too, that he has a Christian vocation. He is called to repentance and to holiness and he hopes to bear the fruit of his Christian vocation in the fruit of the Holy Spirit (Galatians 5:22, 23). The particularity of his personal vocation is implicit in his ministry.

Shortly after George arrived in the parish, a parishioner asked him, 'What sort of cleric are you?'

George did not know how to respond. He wanted to say, 'A very new and somewhat bewildered one!' but he thought better of it. He wondered if the parishioner was alluding to his views or to his stance on a particular matter of faith, doctrine or morals.

Seeing his puzzlement the parishioner continued, '. . . because, in my experience, there are only two kinds of cleric: "workers" and "shirkers"!'

George responded, 'I am a sinner seeking redemption. What kind of parishioner are you?'

How easily, on first meeting someone, do we ask about what they do rather than who they are! We might assume something of their personal qualities from their chosen vocational pathway. Sometimes we would get that right, but sometimes we might get it spectacularly wrong. We might ask a waitress in a restaurant what she did before moving to this country (meanwhile making all sorts of assumptions about her), only to hear that back home she was a consultant paediatrician! Even then, much that she is or has experienced or suffered, much that has shaped her life, is unknown to us.

Our personal vocational pathway is not always characterised by what we have chosen to do or felt drawn to do. Sometimes it has been influenced by what we were driven to do by circumstances. There can be real and continuing inner conflict between doing what we need to do and what we aspire to do. We ask, 'Is this really what God wants me to be doing right now?'

Similarly, we may be conflicted about the person we are and the person we aspire to be. We can carry a burden of guilt because we accuse ourselves of failing to live up to our calling as Christians. We can be acutely aware of our failure to live up to our call to holiness, both in terms of what we choose to do and in terms of what we neglect to do. We all fail to live up to our call to be holy or perfect. It may be of interest that the word 'perfect' in Jesus' words to the rich young man in Matthew 5:48 ('Be perfect, therefore, as your heavenly Father is perfect') is sometimes translated from the Greek as 'complete'. This suggests that, in not fulfilling our vocation, we are incomplete.

Here we might ponder on the relationship of the idea of completion and of fulfilment in vocational terms. As we long for, or strive for, completion and the fulfilment of our human, Christian and personal vocation, we live with the tension between our true call and the denial of our call so that what we do reflects both obedience and disobedience, acceptance and denial, honour and dishonour, grace and sin.

Wrestling with God is the struggle between godliness and sinfulness: conscience being the referee.

The attractiveness of vocational pathways

Do we tend to think of vocation as more than either being or doing something useful or helpful? Do we expect that it is going to have an aura of its own, an aura we desire? If we do, we might be attracted to vocational pathways which seem to us to have an aura about them. It is also possible that we consider that a particular vocational pathway would offer us a cloak of respectability, authenticity or mystical stature. How dangerous that is!

A particular vocational pathway might seem to offer a social status or station in life we might otherwise be denied. Historically this has caused a sharp division between clergy and laity. George, in exercising his gift for flower arranging, sharply divided the congregation between those who felt that it was no occupation for a priest (why wasn't he out visiting the sick?) and those who saw no harm in it. George's skills were a serious threat to some of the members of the church flower-arranging cohort while others thought it was 'nice' that he helped out. The truth of the matter was that while flower arranging had become an important dimension of George's former occupation, it was now such a bone of contention that he decided never to do it again!

Personal call

Keeping in mind the idea that vocation is like a many-faceted diamond, we take a closer look at the work of the Divine Diamond-cutter and reflect next on the detail of our personal call.

The call to become a disciple of Jesus Christ is a very personal one, and no two accounts of how that happened will be the same. Stacey recalls how she was taken by a friend to a Christian festival and was overwhelmed by a sense of the presence of God and became a Christian on the spot! Craig, however, described how he had been going to church with his wife for many years and had experienced nothing of a sense of God until the day his wife said she didn't want to go to church that Sunday. It was then that Craig realised how much he would miss going. A discussion at home made him realise how his life had changed over the years. He began to see how God had been at work in him and he started to let God catch his eye and his ear. A few years later he was ordained a priest.

Personal call includes those occasions when citizens of the world respond to the needs of others in heroic and courageous ways, perhaps going to far-off and dangerous places to give aid to the needy or to rescue the vulnerable. Personal call is also characterised by an appraisal of gifts or skills applied in the service of God and of our neighbour. We understand such gifting as being developmental: not just those gifts we seem to have been born with but the skills and talents we have developed through training and education, through life experience, through tragedy and through the building-up of confidence. It all adds up to a new and a becoming personal call. How often one hears people who are on the threshold of a new route to their vocational pathway declare that even five years before they could not have offered what they now can offer! Here they acknowledge the hand of God, the Divine Diamond-cutter, shaping their life for his greater glory and for the benefit of others.

Pause for reflection

Reflect for a few moments on your personal vocation and how it has been shaped. How different are you from a few years ago?

Christ-centred vocation

If we go around looking at churches, reading their noticeboards, or we scan their websites, we can pick up a sense of what is important to that church, to its leaders and congregation. We will pick up something of their mission or their outreach as well as something of their style of worship.

Tamsin left home for university and sought a church for worship and fellowship. She scanned the noticeboards outside a number of neighbouring churches before telephoning home for advice on what was really being presented on the noticeboards. Words like 'open', 'Bible-believing', 'inclusive' or 'traditional' could all be interpreted in a number of ways. Perhaps it was a code for the initiated, like the sign of the fish on the doorposts of first-century Christians. Reading between the lines, Tamsin picked up that some churches seemed to be suggesting that before belonging one had to accept certain beliefs, lifestyle or standard of behaviour. Others seemed to offer unconditional belonging, with belief, lifestyle and behavioural changes to come out of belonging. These she found more attractive.

Christ is central to Tamsin's life, and belonging in Christ is the foundation of her vocation. She understands herself to be called, as St Paul puts it, to 'belong to Jesus Christ' (Romans 1:6). Does not Tamsin speak for us all? Our primary and foundational call is to belong to Christ. It is in this context that we are called to be 'saints' (Romans 1:7). What we are called to do, how we live and how we behave, all come out of our primary call to belong to Christ.

The contemporary Church and vocation

Published in 1989, 'Call to Order: Vocation and Ministry in the Church of England' is the report of a working party which set out to describe and define the Church's understanding of vocation. The working party admits that in the Church of England there have been different emphases on vocation but that at the time of the publishing of their report it was commonly assumed that to encourage vocations was to encourage candidates for ordained ministry.

The report goes on to quote from the Book of Common Prayer ordinal, reminding us that the prospective deacon is asked if they understand their call as coming from the Holy Ghost, and making the link between personal inner call and public recognition of that call. The report asserts that the Church's policy on vocation has to find a balance between understanding 'call' as personal and understanding it as a call within the community of the Church. A policy with too much emphasis on personal call, maintains the report, is in danger of ignoring necessary interaction between the individual and the community, and of neglecting the premise that the vocations of all God's people are inter-related. Further, the working party assert that to hold a view that only those who are ordained have a vocation is to bring a sense of the ordained having a higher status in the Church than the laity. They make the point, too, that an over-emphasis on individual vocation actually detracts from the vocation of the whole community of the baptised people of God. In strong terms, the report emphasises that vocation is for all. Indeed, many contemporary writers on the subject make the same point in an attempt to rectify the exclusivity of vocation as it had become by the beginning of the twentieth century.

Although authorities generally agree on the drift towards the understanding of vocation as the exclusive province of clergy and vowed religious, we cannot hold that everyone thought that way until recently. The eighteenth-century Welsh-born English poet, orator and Anglican priest George Herbert, for example, in the words of the hymn 'Teach me, my God and King, in all things thee to see', raises the dignity of basic tasks, when done for the glory of God, to the dignity of vocation:

A servant with this clause (*for thy sake*)
makes drudgery divine:
who sweeps a room, as for thy laws,
makes that and the action fine.[2]

Nor can we assume that all later twentieth- and early twenty-first-century Christians have a broader view of vocation than their predecessors! By no means! The educative process continues. Meanwhile, there are many people who do not appreciate the God-givenness of who they are and what they do (or refrain from doing!).

Vision, vocation and ambition

The aphorism 'A goal without a plan is just a wish' is attributed to the French writer Antoine de Saint-Exupéry (1900–1944). Variations are used widely, especially in the world of personal development and life coaching. It has also acquired a second part: 'A plan without a vision is just drudgery.' Again, one can find an abundance of variations on this aphorism, but the underlying principle remains the same: the connectedness

---

[2]   George Herbert (1593-1633), *Hymns Ancient & Modern, Revised* (William Clowes, 1950), no.337

and interdependence of a vision or goal with the action necessary to achieve it.

In this sense of vocation we hold that God gives us a vision which needs to be attended upon. Such a vision needs to be recognised as being from and of God, and a response is required from us. This is not to downgrade the value of dreams as a means of receiving and appreciating vocation. Far from it! Not only is there biblical precedence for this, but also psychologists would tell us that dreams can reveal matters that are of concern to us but which hitherto have been rooted in our subconscious mind and have been inaccessible. Perhaps we could make a distinction between dreams that are mere wistfulness (we might call them 'pipe dreams') and dreams that are realisable and which galvanise us into action. In the following story we hear how Jenny's pipe dream became a realisable dream, and how it fused wonderfully with a growing sense of her vocation.

Jenny's ambition

Jenny had a dream of owning a little shop selling second-hand goods. It would be a hobby. It would be fun buying things at auctions and smartening them up before selling them on at a profit. It was an idea she had had for more than 20 years but she was never in a position to do anything about it. Through attending auctions she got to know a few people in the trade and was appalled at the mark-up on second-hand goods. For example, an old set of wooden steps (complete with woodworm and bought for a pound at a car-boot sale) was scrubbed down, lime-washed and advertised in the window of a nearby 're-loved furniture' shop as a plant stand, with a price tag of £65! Jenny's vision of the second-hand furniture trade was crumbling.

Then, one Sunday, she heard a sermon about meeting the needs of the poor, and instantly she knew what she was called to do. Using the garage at the side of her home for storage, she began buying up old furniture, restoring it and then offering it to her local social services department and to local charities who helped people to set up a home. She covered the cost of her purchases and materials by running a cake stall at her local church. When they heard of her enterprise, people gave her pieces of furniture that were surplus to requirements, and a retired carpenter offered his help with some of the restoration. Jenny's vision, which included the satisfaction she would get from reviving tired pieces of furniture, married up with her sense of call to help those in need. Vision led to action. Ambition served vocation.

The realisation of Jenny's call to help the needy was not without struggle. There was a mustard seed of an idea but it needed to be developed, and the vehicle for that development was ambition. The vision had to have a plan of action that was within her ethical base and which was doable. It had to capture her imagination and it had to bring a sense of satisfaction and fulfilment. It had to energise her.

Pause for reflection

Do you have a pipe dream? What would it take to make it more than that? Could your pipe dream be Spirit-inspired 'yeast' in the 'bread' of your personal vocation? What might a biographer write about your understanding of your vocation or of your ambitions for God and his kingdom?

The vocations and ambitions of the Conference Four

We left the Conference Four 'Going for God', each according to their understanding of their vocation; each of them interpreting the outworking of their vocation in the light of their gifts, their personality traits and their experience of life in the Church of God. It might be of interest to know what had been in their hearts and minds at the beginning of their discipleship, when each one offered for the ministry that became their life for so long. What did they believe themselves called to be or to do for God, for the Church, for other people, for the kingdom? How would they answer the question, 'What has been your vocation, and what is it now?'

Christine believes she was put on this earth to love God and her neighbour. She holds to the Ten Commandments as written on two large boards in her parish church – one either side of the chancel arch. Every Sunday, as she prayerfully prepares to receive Holy Communion, she reads the list as she reflects on the previous week and brings before God her failings in regard to each one of the commandments. Living out her vocation is, for her, simply a matter of how she lives each day in relation to God and the world about her. She understands her vocation to be to witness to the gospel, the good news of Jesus Christ, as evidenced by her actions rather than her discourse. She believes in 'casserole evangelism' – the leaving of a casserole on the doorstep of a cottage in the village with a card that simply says, 'Thinking of you in your sad loss. I will say a prayer. Love, Christine.' She relies on her association in people's minds with the local church and her promise of prayer to make her point: to witness to her faith. Her vocation as a wife, mother and grandmother as well as an employer is also important to her, and she understands her vocation to be God-given. On occasion she will speak out against injustice, or she will take on an advocacy role for a villager or employee who is in difficulty. She will make a fuss about cuts in local services and, through her charity and committee work, as well as through involvement with church government locally and in a wider context, she will quietly influence policy. She has also been known to broker reconciliation in both secular and church contexts. All this she understands to be her vocation.

Derek, too, is a reconciler, though he would be the first to admit that he dislikes hassle and conflict and likes to get things running smoothly again as soon as possible. He would be hurt by any suggestion that he sees his vocation as maintaining the status quo. It is not that he is against change, but he is suspicious of fads and fashions in church life and needs to understand the reasons for change. He is sympathetic with parishioners who, bewildered by the rapid changes in everyday life, seek solace in the familiarity of church worship. He sees his vocation as being to bring a little sanity to the madness of the Church. He believes he is called to be among his 'flock', to be there in their joys and in their sorrows in the ordinariness of their daily lives. He believes he is called to listen rather than to speak out; to be reliable, steady and solid. He models his Christian discipleship on Jesus and is likely to refer to those times when Jesus did not judge or when he said very little. Central to his vocation is the call to pray for all, to seek out the lost, and to administer the sacraments of the New Covenant.

Ruth would not argue with much of Derek's stance on some things. She, too, dislikes change for change's sake, but when she see that apathy, intransigence and myopia are getting in the way of the kingdom of God, she is ready to do battle. She is likely, however, to use influence rather than authority as a power base. She is a gifted orator, a fine preacher, and can raise levels of enthusiasm in God's people that some only dream of being able to do. She has political nous and chooses her battles carefully. She will take her time and choose her moment to introduce a topic or to startle a dreary meeting with a silver trumpet-like remark that changes the dynamic and moves the meeting on to some sort of resolution. She, too, models her life on that of Jesus and is likely to quote instances of Jesus rescuing those in need or pointing to the plight of the poor. She believes her vocation is to speak out against injustice and to wake up the Church to the needs of the world. Like Derek, prayer is important to Ruth and she regularly brings the needs of the world before God. However, for Ruth, prayer must lead to action. Ruth would say she is not called to be popular but to be effective. She wants to make a difference in the world and, apart from her own direct action, she believes she is called to encourage others to be more proactive in their vocation to bring in the kingdom of God – a kingdom free of poverty, hunger, abuse or oppression.

Hugo is very clear about his vocation. To be fair, Hugo is very clear about everything, and he gets frustrated if others do not share his vision or view of things. Hugo is clear that God gave human beings wits and common sense. He, too, models himself on Jesus and would quote those occasions when Jesus engaged in discourse with his enemies, flooring them with his masterly oration. Hugo marvels at Jesus' ability to outwit his enemies as they tried to trip him up. Hugo is full of God-given energy and imagination. He believes that God has equipped him to build community. He has been tireless in his ministry of breaking down barriers between the 'churched' and the 'unchurched'. The new church school and the reordering of the inside of the church to make it suitable for concerts are both, for Hugo, the fruits of his vocation. For him it is all about 'outreach', and he will cite Jesus on the call to the people beyond the 'holy huddle' of congregants and seeks the provision of facilities that will facilitate relationships and enhance the quality of lives. Somewhat paradoxically, he is single-minded and hates having to work through committees and be subject to rules, regulations, planning permission or Canon Law, and yet he is very good at working through bureaucracy and at rallying support for his cause from among the great and the good of the county and through people of means in both the church and the business world. He says of himself, 'God did not put me on earth to be a wallflower!' His critics might say he is called, rather, to be a thistle under the saddle of life.

The aspect of vocation that requires consideration, not only for the Conference Four but for us all, is that of discerning God's will for us. Our reflections on that will bring us, sooner or later, to some notion of God's purpose, not only for us personally but for all humankind and for the whole of creation. God's purpose is God's ambition, and that is the focus for reflection in the next chapter.

CHAPTER THREE

God's ambition

Leaning in to God's ambition

Before we consider, in the next chapter, the Church's
response to its understanding of God's ambition, we might
find it helpful to address some of the possible dimensions
of that ambition and how we identify them. Here and in
the following chapter, I will use quite often the phrase
'leaning into God's ambition'. I have chosen to use this
phrase because it has a gentleness, a hesitancy and a
diffidence about it.

One thinks of John, 'the beloved disciple', leaning against
Jesus at the last supper (John 13:23). I imagine John listening
to the Lord's heart beating and taking comfort from its
regular and strong beat. Listening with the 'ears' of our heart,
we try to attune our life with God's life. As beloved disciples
ourselves, we sense God calling us to lean into the Divine
Heartbeat. It is a heart that beats with ambition for the world.
Leaning towards the heartbeat of God we are encouraged by
the life we find there. It energises us!

But what shall we do with our energy? Our instinct and
our call is to sense what God wants of us. We cannot know
God in the fullest sense, though we know something of God
from what has been revealed to us – chiefly in Jesus Christ –
and we long to know more and look forward to true intimacy
with God. We love him and long to know him and to serve
him. It is in the desire to serve God out of our great love for
him and for his people that we live as best we can by God's
precepts and do what he wants us to do in so far as we can
understand what is required or requested of us.

Leaning into God's ambition demonstrates a desire to cooperate with God. It is a gesture of consent, and yet it is a hesitancy. It is the leaning into a loved one in the hope of an embrace, but without demanding a response. Leaning in is about taking a risk. Leaning into God's ambition shows a willingness to try to be and to do God's will, and to risk getting it wrong. It is better to lean in, in good faith, and to get it wrong than to be risk averse and to do nothing or to desist from trying to be more faithful. I am using the 'leaning in' metaphor to allow space, but it is a space that is narrowing between us and God – space to allow God to be mysterious and to allow us, as the Church, to have got some things right and some things wrong about God's ambition for the world.

In order to discern a little of what God's ambition might be, we would turn, quite naturally, to the Holy Scriptures, to the place where we would expect to find the revelation of God and his mission, and in particular to those passages that describe the kingdom of God. We look to the Holy Scriptures, too, for guidance regarding our call to holiness and faithfulness as well as a call to make a difference in a real and practical way. Holy Scripture is fundamental to our understanding, but we view it through the lens of more than 2000 years of Christian history and experience of trying to discern God's will, of trying to be obedient, and we view it in the light of developing biblical scholarship, theology and ecclesiology. All this we employ to enable us to discern God's will for us and to enable us to be faithful disciples of our Lord Jesus Christ.

We may hold that God's ambition has a task-oriented intention and is framed, for example, in the words of the angel on the night of our Saviour's birth: 'on earth peace among those whom he favours' (Luke 2:14). Did not the angel declare something of God's ambition on that holy night?

We may want to respond that we cannot possibly know the mind of God: what God truly wants; what God wants to achieve. Perhaps we think it is none of our business! If that is true we might question why God revealed so much of his nature to us, chiefly in the words, actions, life, death and rising of Jesus Christ. For glimpses of God's purpose, God's missional ambition, we may want to be more expansive than that and consider the implications not only of Christ's teaching and the discernment of the early Church as we read it in the New Testament, but also of the early rumblings of the voice of God's ambition as we read it in the Old Testament.

The reflections in this chapter are offered so that the reader might revisit their own opinion about God's ambition and so lean in a little closer, hear more clearly the heartbeat of God and be inspired in discipleship. Christ is central to our faith. He is our faith! His teaching, however, is received by us in many different ways and his presence with us in the Holy Spirit appreciated differently. Together we seek to discover a truth which will unite us.

What we believe about God's ambition

When we seek to examine the possibilities of God's ambition, we need at least two things. First we need to have come to a personal understanding of God: a theology. This is our own 'credo', what we hold and believe about God. A survey of any Christian community or congregation will show that there can be as many theologies as there are community members! The Church worldwide is comprised of denominations, each of which holds a particular view of God and teaches a doctrine that reflects that theology or ecclesiology. Also, the reflections of Christians over two millennia have produced a plethora of opinions that are enshrined in the written works of philosophers, historians, artists and others. A key question for each of us, then, is: 'What do I believe?'

The second thing we need in order to explore God's ambition is a framework that does not circumscribe God – one which doesn't make God too small, too convenient. We need to let God be God, to be essentially unknowable. Yet we need a framework of belief which enables us to focus our discipleship in a manageable way.

As we explore the labyrinths of the mysterious heart of God's ambition, we come to various 'chambers'. For the purposes of this reflection we might find it helpful to explore four such 'chambers' of the vast heart of God. These are:

1. God's ambitious love
2. The Father's creational and re-creational ambition
3. Christ's redemptive ambition
4. The Holy Spirit's ambition to renew the face of the earth.

These four 'chambers' of God's ambitious heart do not claim to represent the whole of that ambition, because to know all of God's ambition would be to presume we know all there is to know about God! The four 'chambers' of the vast heart of God are an attempt to create a framework for an understanding which recognises the over-arching importance of God's love for us, and the remaining three 'chambers' focus our reflections on the God we know in Trinity: Father, Son and Holy Spirit. In terms of the actions of God's love, we might also find it useful to think of the persons of the Holy Trinity in terms of Creator, Redeemer and Sanctifier.

God's ambitious love

How might we respond to the question, 'What is God's ambitious love?' We might want to consider this in a philosophical way, such as God wants to be worshipped and adored, or God wants to be loved in return. I asked Jean, a Christian offering herself for ordained ministry, to sum up her faith in one sentence. Without hesitation, she replied, 'For God so loved the world that he gave his only Son, so that everyone who believes in him may not perish but may have eternal life' (John 3:16).

We might find it difficult to believe that God loves us infinitely and that we are infinitely loveable. It is a love that cannot be fully comprehended, but in so far as we can grasp it, we desire to return it. Love is a dynamic which, to be fully effective and efficacious, requires reciprocation. To stay with the metaphor of the heart, the dynamic of love is the lub-dub, lub-dub of the heartbeat. God loves, lub-dub! Love God, lub-dub!

Loving response

The mystery, the magnitude and the intimacy of being loved and loving back is not where it ends. The love of God in us and for us must spill out in love for our neighbour: it is a call to love those whom God loves. The life-changing, world-changing dynamic at the heart of God's mission is a dynamic of love. Thus we recognise love deep inside us, beyond us, all around us. The adventure of a life lived in awareness of God's love is excited deeply inside us and is expressed dynamically beyond us. We are called to announce the kingdom of God, which is the reign of God's love in the hearts of all, but we announce that kingdom by deed as well as by word, through our acts of love and loving kindness. God's love for us spills out of us in returned love for God and for our neighbour.

In addition to the 'tension' between the God of 'out there' and the God of 'in here', there will be a conduit of desire to embrace both the God of love and love for one's neighbour. There will be a deep-seated care for the needs of others and a desire to share all that we have received from God: our material and spiritual gifting and riches. Together with that striving for intimacy with God, those with a healthy spirituality will know how, or will be open to finding out how, to respond appropriately to the needs of their neighbours. How we make a difference to the lives of others will depend on many things – circumstances, resources, opportunity, gifting – but a person with an authentic spirituality will have the urge to do *something* to help. Here we might reflect on the stark discourse in the New Testament letter of James: 'Faith without works is dead' (James 2:14-26). Our desires will reflect God's desires, and there will be a desire to put love into action.

The Father's creational and re-creational ambition

Reflection on God's creational ambition will depend, to some extent, on how we receive the accounts of creation in the Book of Genesis. Some will receive them as literal accounts – that God made all of creation in six (earth) days. Others will receive them as an attempt by the writers to explain the world around them with its classifications of animals and the status of human beings as having dominion over the rest. There are books aplenty that argue for these, and secular theories about the beginning of time abound, too!

It is not my purpose to explore those arguments here. I ask only that the reader looks about them and marvels at creation. We are all eye witnesses to the wonder of creation. We receive it through our senses as we appreciate life and beauty in its many forms. Through those same senses we also appreciate that many aspects of creation give us cause for concern; they are a threat to our welfare. Fire, for example, is a powerful and awesome thing: it warms us and it cooks our food, but when it is out of control it destroys lives, homes and ancient forests. This reminds us that God's creational ambition is awesome and that we are stewards of his creational wonders, not masters of them.

We may ask ourselves if God's creational ambition was fulfilled at the beginning of time and then he left it to us to be stewards of it, or whether God is still working his purpose out and calling us into cooperation with him in the fulfilling of his ambition. The commissioning of Adam in Genesis 2:15 suggests that part of our human vocation is to take responsibility in the created order. By extension, we understand that our stewardship of the earth embraces everything, including one another – we must not forget to be good stewards of ourselves, too! If this is what we believe, then we begin to glimpse the Church's task in response to God's ambition.

Can we conceive of God's ambition being limited to the re-creation of humankind alone? If not, we can expand our horizons and consider the whole of creation. We might look back to the biblical accounts of creation as reference points, but we might also look beyond those accounts to the possibility of all creation being made new. Now we would have to imagine a world without natural disasters: no more floods, tsunamis or famine. There would be no more buildings struck by lightning and no more deaths as a result. When we consider God's creational ambition, we might imagine God wanting a return to the Garden of Eden idyll, but if God's creational ambition is yet to be fulfilled, we may be awaiting something even better.

Threaded through Scripture are references to a new heaven and new earth. We find the phrase in the prophecy of Isaiah (65:17), in the Second Letter of Peter (2 Peter 3:13) and in the Revelation of John (21:1). There is no doubt that God's people have been looking not only for a future heaven but also for a heaven on earth: a new creation. It is logical to suppose, therefore, that our call to lean into God's ambition for the world is a call to work towards a 'new earth'. People do this in so many ways. Research into the cause and treatment of disease, and technological developments which turn barren places into springs flowing with clean water are just two examples. So what is to come?

Pause for reflection

In terms of a 'new heaven and a new earth', in what ways do you or your congregation lean into God's creative and re-creative ambition?

Christ's redemptive ambition

Here we focus on the centrality of Christ as revealer of God's love, mercy and grace. By his coming among us as a human being, Christ dignifies us, raises us to the status of friends and introduces us to God as a loving parent. However we understand the meaning of the crucifixion, death and resurrection of Christ, the fruit of it is redemption and reconciliation – the promise of new life and hope! But in modelling obedience to our calling, the example of Christ speaks of cost and sacrifice, of laying everything on the line for God. The life, death and rising of Jesus calls for conversion in hearts and lives. It is a call to follow Christ and to emulate him. It is a call to live by the grace of God in obedience even unto death (Philippians 2:8), but with the joyful prospect of new and eternal life to follow!

Adrian's story of his encounter with Christ might help us to reflect on God's redemptive ambition and its relationship to our own.

Adrian received the phone call just before he was about to go on retreat. The voice on the line advised him that the senior ministry team in a neighbouring diocese would be keen to receive from him an application for the post of archdeacon, as currently advertised in the Church press. The message was clear in spite of the somewhat cloaked language: should Adrian apply, he would be offered the post.

Adrian had planned to take some reading with him into retreat: a small collection of books including one or two old favourites and a couple from the top of a pile he had not yet got round to reading. During the week-long retreat he could not settle to read much at all! He found himself, instead, thinking more and more about that phone call. He had not considered himself to be an ambitious person, but rather someone who felt passionately about the role of the Church in contemporary society. He admitted to himself that he had become frustrated of late and felt that he needed more scope to make a difference. Now he was disturbed. Was he being called to the ministry of an archdeacon?

As he stomped somewhat truculently around the grounds of the monastery, Adrian came suddenly upon a life-sized crucifix. The figure of Jesus was depicted as alive and looking down directly at him. He heard a voice ask, 'Are you this ambitious?'

Adrian was so sure he had heard the voice that he swung round to see who had spoken. Still startled, he turned back to the image of Christ crucified and considered the question. He looked at the outstretched arms nailed to the cross. 'No,' he replied, 'I am not *that* ambitious, but I am glad, dear Lord, that you were!'

Adrian knew then that he would apply for the post of archdeacon because he felt he could lean into Christ's ambition for the world through it.

The cross is central to our faith, but when we look upon a symbol of it, what do we understand it to mean? Does it speak of ambitious love? Again, the words of St John put it so well for us:

> For God so loved the world that he gave his only Son, so that everyone who believes in him may not perish but may have eternal life. Indeed, God did not send the Son into the world to condemn the world, but in order that the world might be saved through him.
>
> *John 3:16, 17*

We have gone straight to the heart of God's ambitious and redeeming love, but we can learn even more about God's ambition if we take into account the whole of the Christ event: the birth, life, death and resurrection of our Saviour. We find that it links to God's creational and re-creational ambitions because we no longer simply hold that God created the heavens and the earth and all that is in them, but that God also entered into his creation by becoming human in Jesus. Since that time, creation cannot be the same. The incarnation, the enfleshing of God, changes everything and raises endless possibilities for life to be different. The old order has passed away; behold, a new order is here, turning priorities and hierarchies upside down.

The redemptive work of the cross is accompanied by world-changing possibilities, nothing short of the kingdom of God: God, in Jesus Christ, reigning in all earthly creation as he does in heaven.

The work of redemption might be a finished work, an ambition realised, but the outworking of the significance of God becoming human is an ongoing ambition of God and one we are called to lean into. When Jesus, at synagogue worship, read from the prophecy of Isaiah 61, he took that prophecy to himself and declared that it was fulfilled that day in himself. What a storm that created! In his bold statement he revealed something of God's ambition for the world: 'The Spirit of the Lord is upon me, because he has anointed me to bring good news to the poor. He has sent me to proclaim release to the captives and recovery of sight to the blind, to let the oppressed go free, to proclaim the year of the Lord's favour' (Luke 4:18, 19). Jesus reveals to us something of God's ambition for his kingdom on earth as it is in heaven. Throughout the Gospel accounts, Jesus reveals even more. We think, for example, of his teaching in the words of the Beatitudes in Matthew's account (Matthew 5:3-11).

The doctrine of the kingdom of God should be familiar to us. The kingdom is central to God's plan for the world, but Christians do not have a common mind about it. Some hold that it is something for the distant future while others hold that its coming is imminent. Still others hold that it is a present reality.

We will consider our response to God's kingdom ambitions in the following chapters, and we may find not only that it is a challenging concept but also that individuals, as well as whole church communities, will have their own understanding of it. Experience tells us that it is the cause of bitter disagreement and division in the Church and that some will argue that their own view is the only valid one. Scholars argue that it has never been an easy concept to grasp.

I suggested earlier that Christians today have differing views on the kingdom of God. I am not suggesting that our forebears were any clearer about it! First-century Christians had differing views too, views that were influenced by the culture of the day. Christians came from many different backgrounds: Jews and Gentiles influenced by their religious and cultural heritage. What comes through in reading the New Testament letters, the Acts of the Apostles and the words of Jesus himself is that there was a sense of urgency: that the kingdom was imminent, that it would be life-changing and that it would be a heaven and earth reality in which everything and everyone is redeemable. God's redemptive ambition would win through.

The Holy Spirit's ambition to renew the face of the earth

Beyond salvation through Jesus Christ (as if that were not generous enough!), God holds out an invitation to grow in holiness, to be absorbed into the community of the Holy Trinity. This is possible for us not by any work of our own but by the gift of grace by which we can be transformed. We understand the gifts of the Holy Spirit as not only being given to us individually but also as a dynamic working throughout creation. In the Book of Psalms, and echoed in other parts of Holy Scripture, we are given a glimpse of God's ambition as being to 'renew the face of the earth' (Psalm 104:30, NLT). When that ambition is fulfilled, we will see and experience the fruit of the Spirit in all of humankind as listed in Galatians 5 – in love, joy, peace, patience, kindness, generosity, faithfulness, gentleness and self-control. The renewal of the face of the earth is nothing short of the establishment, in holiness, of the kingdom of God on earth. This is what the Bible teaches us is the ambition of God, which is to be achieved by the power of the Holy Spirit: 'to renew the face of the earth'. When we look about us we may notice signs of such a renewal while lamenting that there seems to be a long way to go!

Part of our call to greatness is the enormous privilege of being vessels of God's grace, filled as we are with so many gifts, Christ himself ministering his grace through us! Whatever we think about the kingdom, the gifts of the Holy Spirit are for now and for the transformation of the world. These gifts, poured out in the Church from the Day of Pentecost onwards, are the very life of God at work among us and through us to the whole world. By discerning, recognising and using our gifts, we cooperate in God's ambition to renew the face of the earth. We exercise our gifts in modesty and humility but also with authority. It is the authority of Jesus given to us by him. The outpouring of the Holy Spirit shows us just how God intends to fulfil his ambition in re-creative, redemptive and sanctification terms.

God's ambition and the revelation of the kingdom

The Bible gives us many insights into God's ambition, whether that be creative and re-creative, redemptive or gloriously power-filled renewal in the Spirit. There is one passage on which I would like us to reflect before we move on to consider the Church's response to God's ambition. For me, it is an excellent example of God's ambition in terms of the kingdom of God on earth as it is in heaven. I am thinking of the second chapter of St John's Gospel.

After the wonderful account in chapter one of how God came to earth in Jesus, the Word made flesh, John goes straight to a revelation of God's power and intent in the story of the marriage feast at Cana in Galilee. This story has become popular as a reading at weddings because the presence of Jesus at the feast appears to endorse the institution of marriage (and maybe to endorse the party that takes place afterwards!). I think St John would be most disappointed, however, if we did not pick up his deeper theological meaning in this story.

We remember that, unlike the other three Gospel accounts, John is not writing a narrative of the events of the life of Jesus, as such. He chooses what he includes in order to underline what he believes and what the Christian communities for whom he writes have also come to believe.

For John, Jesus is the revelation of God. Jesus is Emmanuel, God with us! In the story of the wedding feast at Cana, John wants us to know that Jesus has the power of God. He is already King of earth even as he is King of heaven. In this passage, John makes a royal proclamation of ascent. It would be followed later by the royal coronation which would take place, paradoxically, on the cross in the sacrifice of Jesus' life.

Scholars tell us of the importance of a wedding celebration to the people of Jesus' time: how it would go on for days, and how important hospitality was on the part of the bridegroom. In this story, the bridegroom is embarrassed because the wine has run out. Jesus is heralded into the manifestation of divinity by his mother Mary who tells him of the bridegroom's plight. Jesus appears offhand in his response. He is coy about what he can do about the problem. Mary, who knows him so well and whose own life experiences have given her inside knowledge of her son's true identity, simply tells the servants to do what Jesus tells them to do. This instruction alone would be a good place to begin our response to our insights into God's ambition. We could do worse than simply do what Jesus tells us to do! At a word from Jesus, enormous pots of water are found to be filled with wine – and not just any old wine but good wine: the best!

Created matter, plain water, at the word of Jesus is 'redeemed' as wine. In this miracle, Jesus demonstrates more than rescue of an embarrassed bridegroom or the amazement of bewildered servants. Jesus demonstrates the lavish and overwhelming generosity of God in the face of human need. Jesus manifests, shows to the world, the generous and limitless (there was so much wine it might as well have been limitless!) love of God for his people. Jesus shows God's dominion over created matter. It is an act of God in human circumstance.

'Your kingdom come ...'

If we ask Christians what they understand the kingdom of God to be about, we get a range of answers. For some, God's ambition is to love everyone into the kingdom no matter how long that takes: an endeavour which continues after earthly life. For others, it is the establishment of the rule of Christ as King of heaven and King of earth and is based on biblical teaching on grace, salvation and judgement. There is a sharp divide between those who will be part of the kingdom and those who won't. For still others, it is the establishment of a kingdom on earth where hunger and poverty are no more: a kingdom of justice, equity and peace. Still others say they would like less clear demarcation, or 'the kingdom' means something different altogether.

I don't intend to judge which vision of the kingdom of God is the correct one but rather to ask the reader to explore the connection between God's aim and purpose in regard to the kingdom, the everyday 'work' of the Church in relation to it, and the reader's own understanding of what they are called to be and to do with regard to it.

'... on earth as it is in heaven'

What is the nature of the kingdom of God? Is it simply and sublimely that all the souls God created find their way into heavenly bliss? For many of us, holding to that hope is enough to cope with without there being more! But is heaven our final destination?

The understanding of the first Christians, as ratified in the Nicene Creed, is that there is more to the kingdom of God than a spiritual and celestial realm; that the kingdom of heaven becomes the kingdom of earth because the same king rules over all. There is no divide between the two. If we truly believe that, it not only colours the expansiveness of God's ambition but also indicates how we are to live now and how we are to announce and to proclaim the kingdom.

It also raises questions about the role of the Church in cooperation with God's plan to usher in that kingdom. Are we to be the 'womb' of the kingdom or the 'midwife' of it? We may wonder if God's re-creational ambition is merely a kingdom which is a spiritual domain beyond our present life, or perhaps a cosmic domain with relocation somewhere in the universe, somewhere beyond planet earth: a place to go to get away from the disasters that beset God's people.

Towards the end of the Nicene Creed we state our belief in the 'life of the world to come'. Do we understand that world as being another 'world', or do we understand it as a new life in this world: a world transformed – a place free of disease or pollution, for example? If we unpack our deep aspirations for the coming of the kingdom, we begin to ponder on what that kingdom is or will be like. We make assumptions about it, some of which inform us as to where our own difficulties lie.

One kingdom, one king

Finally, does our imagining of the kingdom move our focus on a 'place', a paradigm for a better way of life, to a focus on the King of heaven and earth, to Jesus Christ as the 'place' of the kingdom? If we can make that shift of focus, we will begin to envisage the kingdom to be more than God's ambition for a better way of life for all. The kingdom will be for us a 'place' where God reigns, and further, it is the 'place' where God is. The kingdom will be nothing short of an attribute of God! God's ambition, then, is to be God of all. God's ambitious love is God's mission to the world.

Pause for reflection

What is the kingdom of God like? Imagine its structures and its people. Do they represent both genders, all ethnic origins, all sexual orientations? Are there people of faiths other than Christianity, or people of no faith at all?

A key reflection for us concerns whether or not we can recognise when informed assumptions about God's ambitions are shared, and to consider what we do if they are *not* shared but imposed upon us. If you were to share with others your thoughts about the nature of the kingdom of God, would there be disagreement among you?

We reflect, in the following chapter, on the role of the Church in relation to that kingdom and missional ambition.

CHAPTER FOUR

Whose kingdom? The Church's response to God's ambition

Listening to people's aspirations for the world, for life in general or for themselves one hears so often that people just want to make a difference. This desire is the energy behind research which seeks to resolve problems such as disease, poverty or conflict. It is this desire which drives some to give up everything and to go to far flung places in response to some new disaster. Is there, too, a desire for greatness? Sometimes the answer is 'yes'. Does every new politician have nothing but the desire to make a difference in society or is there something of a desire for fame? Perhaps that comes later in the heady days of power and authority. Perhaps it simply comes with the territory.

In following our desire to make a difference we consider many things. We ask what our options might be. We ask how best to go about making a difference and what our contribution might be. We are less likely to begin our interior dialogue with: 'How can I achieve greatness?' Yet, greatness may well follow our dedication to making a difference. So, what is greatness?

I suggest that, in this, we are responders rather than initiators, though we might like to believe otherwise. We respond to God, who has called us into life and into new life in Jesus Christ. Our life is rooted in God's life; our purpose rooted in God's purpose. Our vocation is lived expression of God's call. Our call to greatness is a response to God's greatness and to God's ambition.

Perhaps the reader is more comfortable with the word 'mission' than the word 'ambition'? Yet is not the 'A' word redeemed somewhat when it evokes thoughts of God's mission being fulfilled in all creation? So interconnected is the one to the other that I like to refer to the phenomenon as *Ambmission.*

Discerning God's mission, God's ambitions for a situation, place or circumstance, is not always easy. There will be those who will tell us categorically what God wills or wants for his people or for the planet, but sometimes we hear contradictory accounts of God's will and purpose which serve to confuse us or to cause us to despair of knowing the truth. Such despair can bring some Christians to the point of giving up trying to discern God's will altogether.

'Thy kingdom come'

When Jesus' disciples asked him to teach them how to pray he gave them a series of phrases we know as the Lord's Prayer (Matthew 6:9-13). At the heart of them is, 'Thy kingdom come.' Every time we pray that we express our aspirations for its establishment, but what goes through our mind as we pray those words? To pray this phrase is to acknowledge God's ambition. When we pray it we express our own aspiration for the coming of that kingdom. Thus by that aspirational phrase we lean in to God's ambition: we associate ourselves with it. Deep within ourselves, and even without unpacking the Lord's design for the kingdom, we acknowledge it.

God's ambition and God's mission of love

God's missional love *is* God, who is love. The kingdom of God declared by Jesus is Jesus himself, present for all time and eternity as King of love. The Church is called to announce, to participate in and to model God's love. All that we are, all that we do and all that we have is at the disposal of God's mission of love. One approach to our response to God's ambition, therefore, is to ask ourselves, in regard to everything we do, 'Is Love served by this action?'

It is not uncommon to hear of the Church's mission to the world as if it is something we do on God's behalf. The reality is that it is God's mission to the world: we being participators in the fulfilment of that mission. God's mission is not limited by the boundaries of the Christian Church. God's mission is one which embraces all people of goodwill. Now we draw closer to the truth of the matter. It is not our mission. What we are about is allowing, facilitating and cooperating with God whose mission it is! The very least the Church could do is to not get in the way of God's missional work. Self-serving ambition, which we shall explore more fully in later chapters, does precisely that!

We might be forgiven if, by this stage of our reflection, the establishment of the kingdom of God seems unattainable, not least because we may believe that the Church could not possibly have a common mind about it! Being overwhelmed about the kingdom and our seemingly small personal part to play in announcing it or forwarding it, we might be inclined to give up thinking about it or even despair of the kingdom ever coming! We should not allow ourselves such despondency. First of all, God's ambition will be fulfilled. Secondly, we are called, for the most part, simply to be obedient to our own vocation within God's greater ambition. Thirdly, there are dangers in the people of God being complacent about the nature of the kingdom and of the Church's role in it, but we should not underestimate the action of the Holy Spirit in energising us, guiding us and enabling us.

In discerning what the Holy Spirit is doing among us, we need to regularly and routinely seek to link the activity of the Church to what we understand God's ambition to be. Discerning what God's Spirit is doing is a corporate as well as an individual endeavour. It involves us asking questions of ourselves, of one another and – especially – of those who lead us. If we cannot ask searching questions of our leadership, there is something seriously wrong with the climate or culture of our church. Leaders should be able to answer questions about how what they call us to be or to do fits in with God's ambition. If we cannot ask such questions and receive answers which address our concerns, we will allow ourselves to follow 'false prophets' and self-serving individuals, to the detriment of the kingdom.

If there is to be any blame here, it rests on the whole people of God: both those who lead us astray and we who have allowed ourselves to be led astray. The same premise applies to situations where we are not being led anywhere at all, where complacency has crept into leadership. Some leaders will complain that while they once had energy, zeal and imagination for kingdom-building initiatives, they have come up against a wall of apathy or sabotage. A 'them and us' culture in the Church is to be deplored, but we might sympathise with those who began their ministry with energy and zeal and who have been worn down by inertia or resistance to change. This has caused some leaders to give up and to settle for trying to maintain the status quo. Similarly, inertia and resistance to change among church leaders has led congregants to move to another congregation or denomination, while others have given up attending church altogether.

No task too great

We should acknowledge, however, the awesomeness and the scale of God's ambition. This is the God whose declared intention is to 'renew the face of the earth' (Psalm 104:30)! Renewing the face of the earth does seem rather daunting. Perhaps this personal story might help:

My wife and I took the bold step of getting rid of the cream carpet in our dining room and replacing it with patterned charcoal-grey vinyl floor covering. The carpet created endless work to keep clean what, in summer, is a thoroughfare to the garden. We spent two years talking about it. Would the choice of vinyl make the room dark or would it bring the pale beech furniture to life? Would there be enough light in the room to carry the darker floor? Would the sheen on the vinyl bring more light rather than less? These were some of the questions in our minds. We decided that floor covering is not for life (though we hope this will see us out), and so finally we took the plunge.

We were in and out of the carpet store in ten minutes flat! The project took a week to complete as we had to empty the room (vowing to get rid of too much china acquired over years in ministry). Two men came and boarded the floor, hammered and banged and finally laid the vinyl. Everything had to be put back and lamp wires had to be hidden; we needed a few new bits and pieces to complete the makeover, and finally we enjoyed a meal in the new dining room to celebrate.

It occurred to us, if it took us two years and much deliberation and labour to renew the face of the dining room floor, just how much effort does it take to renew the face of the earth? Perhaps the task of helping the Spirit to renew the face of the earth is so daunting that we plead our case to do nothing. We may hear, 'I am tired, clapped out; I've seen it all before. I only come to church to have a private moment with a private God.' But if not us, then who?

Even if we are ready, willing and able to play our part in God's mission, we may still be confused about the nature of that mission. We may be aware that even in our own church congregation or community there are widely differing views, not only of the nature of the kingdom but also of what we should be doing to cooperate in the announcement of that kingdom.

Differing models of God's mission and the Church's response

Perhaps we might be more enthusiastic about playing our part in God's mission if only we could all agree on what God is expecting of us! God's ambition is revealed to us by the life and teaching of Jesus. It is the establishment of the kingdom of God on earth as it is in heaven. How we receive the teaching of Jesus on the kingdom will determine our response. We may hold that the work of the Church is to acquaint the whole world with God's love for all, while endeavouring to demonstrate that love in the way we live with the prospect that God will not rest until he has loved everyone on earth into his kingdom of unconditional love. In this case, all we do would be for the outworking of the dynamic of God's love which turns war into peace, selfishness into generosity, greed into compassion, and through that love there would be a new creation characterised by a global love for God in response to God's love for all. Where we find such love and its outworking, we find the kingdom to be a present reality, and where we hope yet to find it we hold the kingdom as a future prospect. If this is what we believe about the kingdom, then all the Church's resources would need to be focused in the furtherance of such a kingdom.

If, however, we understand the kingdom in terms of conversion to Christianity – a kingdom of the 'saved' alone – we may invest all our resources in initiatives to bring all people to faith, but with scant reference to deepening their faith or encouraging growth in holiness. If we understand the kingdom in terms of Jesus' words about liberation for the oppressed, we may put our energy into social justice initiatives. If we understand the kingdom in terms of the renewal of the whole creation, we may put our energies into conservation.

Perhaps we declare, 'All of the above, please!' Perhaps, for us, these models are interdependent, and so we may come 'full circle' and declare that salvation instils gratitude to God for his love, mercy and grace, and that spills out in love, care and compassion for others – a deep desire to see love conquer all.

Pause for reflection

What does your local church 'say' to the community or to the wider world that the kingdom of God is about? If I were to read your noticeboards or your parish magazine or website, what would it tell me about your understanding of the kingdom of God and about where you focus your human and material resources in response to that?

Whose voice leads the flock?

The position a church community takes on the ambitions of God in terms of the kingdom should determine its local policy and drive its fund-raising and expenditure. So a key question here is: who has the voice of authority in determining the best policy for leaning into God's ambition as you, as a community, have received it?

Whatever response God's people are meant to make, there is a part that, as the Church as a whole, as a local community or as individuals, we are called to play in the fulfilment of God's ambition. Direct divine intervention in the affairs of the world apart (and I don't rule it out!), there is no one but us who is going to announce and forward the kingdom of God. Indeed, Jesus has commissioned us to do so. He has done so in very specific missional terms, such as in his final words to his disciples at the end of St Matthew's Gospel:

> 'Go therefore and make disciples of all nations, baptizing them in the name of the Father and of the Son and of the Holy Spirit, and teaching them to obey everything that I have commanded you. And remember, I am with you always, to the end of the age.'
>
> *Matthew 28:19, 20*

These words of Christ are sometimes called 'The Great Commission' or 'the New Creation Mandate'. By these words, Christ calls his disciples to witness to the gospel to the ends of the earth. This was their commissioning – and it is ours, too.

Jesus teaches us, too, about care and compassion for those in need – for example, in the parable of the final judgement (Matthew 25:31-46). These remits are awesome, and somewhat daunting, but if not us, then who else is going to cooperate with God in fulfilling these commands? More than that, and keeping in mind our reflection on vocation in an earlier chapter, we may each dare to ask ourselves what am *I* called to be and to do in relation to these commands? In other words, how is *my* ambitiousness (itself a gift from God) to be put to the service of God? Our initial response, in accordance with the reflection above, is that we are called to love God and to love our neighbour as ourselves and to declare that everything else is an outworking of obedience to that call. As we noted previously, this is not *our* mission but God's mission: it is missional love.

We have explored God's mission in terms of the divine ambition. So far so good! We have explored how our personal vocation leans into that ambition. There is a further step to be made. The writer of the Letter to the Ephesians reminds us that God has 'knitted together' our vocational gifts: 'from whom the whole body, joined and knitted together by every ligament with which it is equipped, as each part is working properly, promotes the body's growth in building itself up in love' (Ephesians 4:16). The fulfilling of God's ambitious and missional purpose requires us to cooperate and to collaborate with one another. Here I suggest that such collaboration extends beyond the structures and frameworks of the Christian Church to working with all people of goodwill for the good of the whole creation.

Perhaps our reflection on the level of agreement on the ambitions of God and the nature of the kingdom of God in our local community offers us clues – concerns even – about the level of agreement in the worldwide Church. We might have concerns, too, about what dangers or difficulties arise from disunity on these matters. We may be challenged by how easy it can be for a local church, a denomination or an individual to over-focus on one vision to the exclusion of a wider vision of the kingdom. Perhaps we believe it is of no great importance that there is divergence of opinion; we may feel that our diversity enriches the Church and does not cause confusion or scandal to those seeking God. There is no doubt that the Church as a whole does spend a lot of time and energy in seeking to appreciate difference, in honouring diversity and in debating how best to serve God and neighbour, but we continue to be seekers after truth on matters of God's missional love, and many unchurched people are confused and scandalised by our internal warfare. Some within the Church may believe that the ongoing debate is pointless and a waste of time, and are tempted to stride ahead unilaterally. This gives opportunity to self-serving ambition. Wherever there is a multiplicity of models, it is easy for a self-serving person to argue that their own model is the only correct one. 'After all,' they will argue, 'as there are so many models claiming to be the right one, why should mine not be the true one?'

We cannot, of course, do nothing in the face of a world in need of God's love, mercy and grace. We cannot say nothing for fear of not saying exactly the right thing in every circumstance. We must listen to the voice deep within us and take such action as seems best to us. However, as any member of any church committee or council will know, endless procrastination is demoralising and debilitating. Over and against a culture or climate of indecision regarding how best to be obedient to God's call to announce the kingdom by deed and word is the danger that the clear, strong voice of an individual can sound like wisdom. There are dangers when that voice is accompanied by a forceful personality, when it comes in the form of unchallenged authority and is set in a context of a powerless community without a voice. What happens when a particular 'brand' of God's kingdom ambition is subsumed to the ambitions of individuals – particularly those in positions of authority and leadership in the Church?

Biblical browbeating and institutional bullying

We are familiar with the way that Holy Scripture is used (and abused) in order to promote a particular stance on almost any matter. In the same way, the earnest direction of an individual, or a group of individuals, can steamroll a church congregation or community into believing that the kingdom of God is characterised in such and such a way without consultation, discussion or consensus, in a way that the early Church would not recognise. Through organisational and institutional bullying, human and material resources can be subverted to the fulfilment of self-serving ambition.

Perhaps the reader has experienced even some laudable ambitions being worked out by egotistical individuals and is aware that some laudable ambitions, no matter how sensitively handled, occasion pain and suffering for some people both inside the Church and beyond it. Perhaps we have all experienced the situation of a great idea badly handled. There is no doubt that some church initiatives, purportedly projects which lean into God's ambition, carry significant risk to health and life. When individuals lose everything for the sake of the kingdom we proclaim them martyrs and thank God for their courage, their self-sacrifice and their witness. When individuals lose everything under misguided and self-serving leadership we call them victims. The problem is that it is not always clear which scenario is which!

We may well ask ourselves what is the place of collateral damage in the outworking of ambition. We may ask how we can tell the difference between God-inspired ambition and egotistical ambition, and what we can do to foster the former and to bring into check the latter. These are matters for reflection in later chapters.

Ambitious love and deep desire

First response

Our first response to God's ambitious love is to desire to love God in return and to share our experience of God's love with the whole world. We associate love with desire in relation to God. We desire an intimate relationship with God. In this, we desire what God desires. We desire to share the love of God with others. We desire to make it known to the world that God loves us all and that we are all infinitely loveable.

How often do we share with one another our deepest desires for the kingdom of God? Perhaps we do so implicitly. Do we think of it as 'a given'? Do we hear the voice of the member of our church council or committee who cries out in frustration, 'May we not speak of God and God's mission of love in the midst of all this talk about the bell tower or whether there should be biscuits with the coffee after Sunday worship?' Does that person embarrass us?

Pause for reflection

When did you become aware of God's love for you? What does that awareness motivate you to do? How long is it since you have shared your thoughts about God's missional love with others and pooled ideas for the sharing of God's love with those around you?

Second response

The second response of the Church is to express gratitude for creation, for salvation and for grace. Gratitude is the appropriate response to grace. Both words stem from the same source and should be understood as reciprocal. Deep gratitude engenders wonder, joy, faith and hope; gifts and fruit of God's Holy Spirit.

These Christian characteristics are, themselves, witnesses to God's goodness: such virtues announce the kingdom to those around us. In this sense we are called to be *of* the kingdom rather than to *do* something to build the kingdom. Nevertheless, as individuals and as a Church as a whole, we are called to spread the good news of the kingdom, using words if necessary (as St Francis of Assisi is alleged to have put it).

Telling everyone about the kingdom of God is only part of our calling. We are to evidence the kingdom by the way we live. Thus, every act of kindness evidences the kingdom. Every growth through grief (mourning) to peace and joy evidences the kingdom. The kingdom is evidenced by our aspirations for a better life for all. It is evidenced through our hope and optimism for the resolution of the world's ills. It is evidenced through our vision and imagination and the commitment we have to the realisation of our God-given visions. Even if our energies are low or our morale has plummeted and our optimism has given way to pessimism, we evidence the kingdom by our longing for it. What we long for, we unself consciously hope to achieve.

Salvation will always mean more to us than conversion, more than making disciples. It will extend, in the root meaning of the word (salve), to wanting to heal and to be healed; to wanting wholeness where there is brokenness, freedom where there is oppression, life where there is death.

Announcing, proclaiming and telling everyone the news that the kingdom of God has come will always be more than vocal rhetoric, oration or preaching. Words without actions will bring nothing about, but action often begins with an exchange of words – sometimes angry words – as issues of injustice are voiced and protests are made. Words inspire action. When I was ordained, a friend of mine gave me a little card on which were printed these words: 'When I give food to the poor, they call me a saint. When I ask why the poor have no food, they call me a communist.'[3] For Christians – indeed, for humankind as a whole – feeding the hungry and at the same time asking why they have no food is entirely appropriate.

Seeking and finding the kingdom of God is done not so much through a telescope which shows the minutest detail in spectacular clarity. It is more like looking through a kaleidoscope, where a myriad of colours form endlessly changing beautiful patterns.

In every generation, the Church has sought to follow its Master and to be obedient to his call to announce the good news of the kingdom. Each generation has brought new challenges, both internally to the Church's governance and externally to its response in deed as well as word to the needs of the world. Each of us could list the challenges facing the Church in our own generation. Each church community or congregation will weigh and debate what needs to be done to lean into God's ambition in terms of the kingdom and how best to use all that God has provided for the purpose. Each one of us needs to regularly review how we are responding to God's call and how we are using in God's service his gifts to us. We are getting there, but we are a divine and great work in progress. The German Catholic philosopher Josef Pieper uses the term *viator* (meaning 'wanderer, walker, wayfarer, pilgrim').[4] He reminds us that we speak of our earthly life as a pilgrimage and says that this is a perfectly honourable and legitimate use of the word. Pieper understands us to be a people who are 'not-yet'. We are 'on the way'. We are becoming. This should give us hope when the reality of our

---

[3]   Dom Helder Camara, former Brazilian Archbishop.
[4]   J. Pieper, *Death and Immortality* (Indiana: St Augustine's Press, 1968), p.73.

response to God's call is less then we might like, whether that call be to the whole Church or to us individually.

Models of the kingdom and paradigms of kingdom living are patterns for possibility, but 'we have this treasure in clay jars, so that it may be made clear that this extraordinary power belongs to God and does not come from us' (2 Corinthians 4:7). Paradigms apart, then, it is through us human beings that God has chosen to announce his kingdom. He has graced us and gifted us fragile human beings who live in the messiness of everyday life. He helps us on our way as we seek to make sense of what and who we encounter, as we live with unanswered questions and, indeed, at times do not know which questions to ask!

In the following chapter we explore further how God's ambitions are worked out in and through a people who are on their way but not yet there.

CHAPTER FIVE

God's ambitious creatures: great and small

Christ has no body but yours,
no hands, no feet on earth but yours.
Yours are the eyes with which he looks
compassion on this world.
Yours are the feet with which he walks to do good,
yours are the hands with which he blesses all the world.
Yours are the hands, yours are the feet,
yours are the eyes, you are his body.
Christ has no body now but yours,
no hands, no feet on earth but yours.
Yours are the eyes with which he looks
compassion on this world.
Christ has no body now on earth but yours.

Those words, attributed to St Teresa of Avila (1515–1582), remind us that, following the Ascension of Christ into heaven and the coming of the Holy Spirit at Pentecost, the fulfilment of God's ambition (whatever we decide that is!) is going to be through fragile human beings like you and me. We may have laboured for years in the service of God, and as we have got older we may have become more conscious of our fragility. Perhaps life experiences have changed what we believe about God and the kingdom. We may have mellowed in our views as real issues faced by real people have challenged the rhetoric we received long ago. We are still on the path of the *viator* and perhaps what we can now offer to God is markedly different from what we have offered in the past.

Perhaps Sister Evangeline's story might illustrate this:

Sister Evangeline, a very elderly nun, had in her younger days lived and ministered in some of the most difficult and dangerous places in the world. She had taught catechism to countless Christian converts as well as binding up their wounds and fighting their corner against the forces of totalitarian authorities. While having her feet washed by Sister Pauline she remarked, 'I once had pretty feet but now they are old and ugly and, like the rest of me, rather worn out!' Sister Evangeline looked down at her hands and remarked that the same could be said of those. With the words of St Teresa in mind she asked Sister Pauline what use she could now be to Christ and his mission.

Sister Pauline smiled, kissed Sister Evangeline's feet and responded, 'Christ has been ever present in these feet and hands and is present still. Now your work is to pray to the Father even as Christ did.'

What we do for God changes both with our developing ideas about God and with our changes of circumstance. Our vocation is not static. It evolves, and so there is a need to continue to listen with the 'ears' of our heart, to keep retuning to the heartbeat of God as we lean ever closer to him.

Guidance comes in many forms and includes those who have seen potential in us for a particular work, service or ministry. Such people will not be unaware of our shortcomings, our fragility. God will not try us beyond our strength, so our fellow human beings ought not to do so either! However, those who guide us or lead us are also fragile human beings and they are capable of exploiting us, bullying us or undermining our confidence in many different ways. We could say that we should not allow them to treat us so, but sometimes that is easier said than done.

It is difficult to estimate whether such abuse is more prevalent within the Church than beyond it. Human beings are the same everywhere, but there is a sense in which we expect to practise what we preach and to behave in a more Christ-like way towards one another. Christians behaving badly make for juicy stories of scandal in the tabloid press!

Perhaps the reader has, like me, worked in secular employment and has been tempted to compare how people are treated in the workplace with how people are treated within the structures of the Church. Perhaps, like me, the reader has encountered pastorally sensitive employers; supportive, open and honest colleagues; and workplace policies that pledge to enable employees to reach their full potential through programmes of development and opportunities for playing a fuller part in the aims of the organisation. We could consider the service industries here rather than the commercial ones if that is too much of a leap into the unknown. Some service industries exploit their workforce abominably, but others do not. Industries which provide food, shelter, medicine, healthcare and treatment, and education are making a difference in the world. Christ has no hands or feet but theirs!

I recall interviewing a bright and able young staff nurse (I was Senior Nurse and Manager of a hospice at the time). I asked him where he saw himself five years hence. He replied, 'Doing your job!' Indeed, he *was* doing my job, and in less time than that! I have followed his career in healthcare over the past three decades and have seen him retire from a very senior role. During those decades he has championed tirelessly the needs of the sick and the disabled. He has made a difference, and his ambition did not get in the way of his achievements but rather gave him the scope he needed to make a greater difference. Christ has no hands or feet but his!

Inspiring as some people might be, we cannot allow too much of a comparison with ourselves. Our supreme example in Christian ministry is Jesus Christ our Lord, and all ministry is to be modelled on his example. We must remember that although we are filled with his Spirit, he is the Emmanuel, the God-made-man. Divine and human and without sin, he is our exemplar; but we need to consider our own frail humanity and our shortcomings with the same compassion with which Jesus regarded his first disciples who, in spite of their many faults, went on to do great things for God.

Greatness and smallness

The amazing achievements of others compared with the perceived inadequacies of our own ministries tend to become synonymous with notions of 'greatness' and 'smallness'. How erroneous and dangerous that is! It is a corruption of something God-given and awesome. It is the deep and fundamental knowledge that greatness, for every one of God's servants, is a dimension of our identity, whereas smallness is the disposition we should adopt if we are to be faithful to our calling to live up to our greatness. Greatness is a gift of God by reason of our participation, at God's invitation, in God's own greatness.

We recognise true greatness in God because he has planted true greatness in each of us! At the same time as we sing in praise of the greatness of God, we place ourselves in smallness before God. Smallness is the disposition we adopt in the face of greatness. It is the disposition of obeisance we adopt in the presence of greatness. Smallness is taking off our shoes for the place where we stand is holy ground (Exodus 3:5). We are in the presence of the greatness of God: a greatness he has shared with us by adoption.

This is how we can reconcile the seemingly irreconcilable. This is how we may make sense of the teaching of Jesus on the subject: 'Unless you change and become like children ... whoever becomes humble like this child is the greatest in the kingdom of heaven' (Matthew 18:1-4). A child is held up as an ideal not because of their innocence but because of their smallness, their humility.

We recall the words of Jesus in Mark's Gospel: 'Whoever wants to be first must be last of all and servant of all' (Mark 9:35). All are 'first' because all are called to greatness, yet all must adopt a disposition of being 'last'. As children of God it is our destiny to be great, but the safeguard against abusing our greatness is the discipline and unrelenting adoption of smallness: always putting others before ourselves.

The Bible and the history of the Church are full of characters who epitomise both greatness and smallness. What do we mean by that? Do we recognise it in other people? Do we recognise it in ourselves? Perhaps such people are truly humble. The author of *The Cloud of Unknowing* writes of humility:

> Let us take a look first of all at humility. We shall see that it is 'imperfect' when it springs from mixed motives, even if God be its chief reason; and that it is 'perfect' when it is caused solely by God. In the first place we must know what humility is if we are to understand it properly: then we may be able to assess more truly what is its cause. In itself, humility is nothing else but a true knowledge and awareness of ourself as one really is.[5]

Perhaps those who epitomise greatness in smallness are so confident in their gifts and talents that they can speak of

---

5   C. Wolters (trans), *The Cloud of Unknowing* (London: Penguin, 1961), ch.13, p.70.

them without boasting, without even needing to tag their comments with deference to God. They know, and we know, the source of their greatness! In the simplicity of knowing their greatness they make themselves small, less significant, and so they reflect in their purity and holiness the greater purity and holiness of God. If we say of them that they are wise, they may point us to their foolishness. If we say of them that they are gracious, they may point us to their foibles, but not in ways which deny the truth of either. Such people are not perfect. They are human beings just like us, but they reflect something of the grace of God. They are windows to the Divine. They are like a piece of broken glass on which the sun shines: light is reflected in a rainbow of colours. It makes our heart sing to behold it, but the glass is still broken.

This chapter began with the words of St Teresa of Avila. Her life and ministry of reform will be known to some, although not to all, but she is better known than some of those we call 'saints'. Perhaps there is insufficient celebration of greatness, of exemplars, in our time. Perhaps we are afraid something may be lost by the open acclamation of achievement based on what we might call laudable ambition. Some ministries, by their nature, are hidden and there is no way to acclaim them. Perhaps that is for the best. We might recall, however, the words of Jesus that there is nothing hidden that will not be disclosed (Mark 4:22), but must that truism always have a 'day of judgement' and largely negative connotation? It is often cited to refer to wrongdoing or injustice. We seem determined to expose wrongdoing but to keep rightdoing secret! Perhaps we think that to expose it might make the humble proud, or simply make others jealous, and thus we will lose an opportunity for joyous celebration in a spirit of generosity because of envy, resentment or bitterness.

We human beings are rather prone to comparing ourselves one with another. Those exercising ministry in God's Church are no less prone. We may consider ourselves to have few gifts, or we may say that we have lacked opportunity to exercise the few we have. We may consider others to be brighter, quicker or more able for public oratory. We are very good at finding reasons why our ministerial endeavours seem insignificant when compared to those of others. In short, we tend to put ourselves in the 'small' category unless, or until, someone in authority calls us to a position in which we consider ourselves to be among the great and the good. At least that is the illusion. Speak honestly with those who might be regarded as having achieved greatness and it is often the case that they do not see themselves in that way. They may be totally unaware of just how awesome they are! They do not seem to notice what impact their stunning intellect or their amazing gifts of oratory or leadership are having on the Church or the world. Somehow they have remained faithful, humble and holy, and they honestly give God the credit for all that they are and all that they have achieved.

Others may still be harbouring aspirations to greatness: they may have a yearning, a drive that will never be satisfied because they are 'hard-wired' in that way. They are not to be admired as much as to evoke in us a little sadness as we sense they will end their earthly life unfulfilled. Still others are not deluded by grand titles or a higher profile and remain totally fulfilled labouring in the vineyard of the Lord alongside everyone else.

God's creatures:
great and small

To explore further this theme of greatness and smallness I would like to offer the reader a little reflection on two biblical characters. They are quite different one from the other (though they were related!). Their respective roles in the announcement of the kingdom of God were crucial and yet unique.

Mary

The first of the two is Mary the Mother of Jesus. For centuries Mary has been regarded as exemplary. Mary is both great and small. Our reflection on her example of greatness in smallness is viewed through the eyes of an elderly woman, a lifelong Christian, called Sadie.

Sadie nearly always sits in the same pew in church. It is towards the front but over to the side and not far from a window. On the windowsill just above her head is a statue of the Virgin Mary. It is made of glass. I asked Sadie what attracts her to this particular statue. She replied that it makes her think of Jesus. Maybe that is not the answer the reader was expecting but, knowing Sadie, I was not surprised. I asked her to say more about it.

She explained, 'When I come here in the early morning, the cool fresh light from the window makes the statue sparkle like a bubbling stream. It makes me think of the youthful Mary who said "yes" to becoming the mother of the Lord. I think of her simplicity, her trust and her obedience, and I pray I might live my life like that: in simple trust and obedience to Jesus.

'If I come here around the middle of the day, the warm sun strikes the statue and fills it with all the colours of the rainbow. I think of Christ in glory and of what Jesus has promised for all who follow him. The Virgin appears round, strong and mature, and I think about how, by God's grace, we can be strong to face every difficulty as we grow into the measure of the stature of the fullness of Christ (Ephesians 4:13).

'If I come here later in the day, shadows begin to form around the statue, and the crevices in the glass look deeper, like wounds. The smile on the face of Mary is gone and I think of the Passion of Christ and his wounds and all he suffered for us. Then I bring a small candle and place it near the statue. By candlelight the statue radiates warmth and a deep joy in the knowledge of the resurrection of the Lord. I, too, am filled with resurrection joy!

'What I like best about this statue is that Mary is transparent. She does not block our view to Jesus, but rather through her transparency she becomes a lens to show us Jesus in his incarnation, his life, his death, his resurrection and his glorious ascension.'

The greatness in Sadie is also transparently obvious.

John the Baptist

The second biblical character whose life offers us scope for reflection on greatness and smallness is St John the Baptist. Jesus said of him, 'Truly I tell you, among those born of women no one has arisen greater than John the Baptist; yet the least in the kingdom of heaven is greater than he' (Matthew 11:11).

The first time one beholds a knitting pattern it can be quite baffling! It is full of abbreviations such as 'psso, k2tog'. It might as well be in Greek! There are two instructions that are found in many a knitting pattern. They are to 'increase' and to 'decrease', and they bring to mind the words of John the Baptist regarding Jesus: 'He must increase, but I must decrease' (John 3:30). This statement comes at the heart of questions from John's followers about the ministry of Jesus, which they seem to think is rivalling that of John. John the Baptist was charismatic, eccentric, outspoken, straight-speaking and uncompromising. His message was a call to repentance: to turn back to the God of their ancestors and to reject the lifestyle choices of the occupying army and of those who, in the higher echelons of society, colluded with their waywardness.

John had a large following of people whose hopes were pinned on him for their rescue from oppression. His significant following was also a serious threat to the ruling body who would have had spies everywhere to watch for any signs of insurrection. Indeed, Herod had held off doing anything about John because he was afraid of a riot.

It was all the more surprising to his followers, therefore, that John was pointing away from himself and towards Jesus as the one they should follow. How often does a leader do that? 'Don't follow me but follow him or her!' John the Baptist knew that his role was to make way for the coming of the Messiah: someone who, as his kinsman, he had known all his life. Their birthdays were only a few months apart. We remember that on hearing of the news of the indwelling of our Saviour in his mother Mary's womb, the unborn John leapt in the womb of his mother Elizabeth (Luke 1:44).

St John the Evangelist is the only Gospel writer to record those words of John the Baptist: 'He must increase, but I must decrease.' As we noted in an earlier chapter, John the Evangelist is not intent on writing a narrative of the events of Christ's life, death and resurrection; rather he is making a number of theological points on which we are to ponder, where we can discover layer upon layer of meaning, and decipher coded language (rather like reading a knitting pattern!).

In that statement alone by John the Baptist we have scope for reflection on greatness and smallness. For John the Evangelist, Jesus is the awesome Word made flesh, God incarnate. When he records John the Baptist as pointing away from himself and towards Jesus, rendering himself small and insignificant in relation to Jesus, he is reminding us that Jesus is much more than another itinerant preacher. It is as if John is saying, 'There is your Messiah but don't limit yourselves even to that. There is your God! He is the Lamb of God: the one who will be the ultimate Passover sacrifice. There is the one to follow because he is God incarnate, and of the increase of God there is no end.' It is so like John the Evangelist to make the link between the words of John the Baptist as herald and forerunner and Christ who would be the ultimate Passover sacrificial lamb!

If an iconographer were to write an icon of the scene of Jesus and John the Baptist together, the image of Christ would be large and the image of John very small. It would be a bit like Graham Sutherland's tapestry in Coventry Cathedral which depicts the enormous enthroned Christ in glory and a life-sized figure of a human being between Christ's feet.

There are parallels for us in life today. Christians, as well as others, still have an uncomfortable message for rulers and governments about the way they treat people or about their lifestyle or environmental choices. We have many charismatic Church leaders, in all denominations around the world, many of whom have a personal following that numbers in the thousands. In the history of the Church there have always been individuals who have spoken out against injustice or oppression. Martin Luther King Junior (1929–1968) is one example. There have always been those who have reformed what needed reforming, but the most exemplary models have always pointed away from themselves and towards God or the needs of others. The words of John the Baptist can be, for us, a mantra: 'He must increase; we must decrease.'

In our everyday lives and ministries it is very easy to self-aggrandise. In modern parlance, we might 'big ourselves up':

draw attention to ourselves or strut about in the office we hold in the Church. Imagine a Church which modelled itself on the example of John the Baptist, a Church whose members pointed away from themselves to Christ (the true model of all our ministries). Imagine a Church where every member lived the mantra, 'He must increase as I must decrease.'

The message and the messenger

Following the account in St John's Gospel of Jesus washing the feet of his disciples (John 13:3-17) there comes a discourse about servants and masters. One function of a servant in that society was to deliver messages for their master. From the words of Jesus we can deduce that his meaning is that the messenger is never more important than the message. The bringer of news should never be more important than the news. People who tease us with, 'I have good news and I have bad news. Which do you want first?' immediately make themselves (the messenger) more important than the message!

We may hold that all Scripture, though divinely inspired, is interpreted by human beings. We become messengers of the message and sometimes, to a greater or lesser degree, we get in the way of the message. We are capable of obscuring the message. In contemporary Church debates one hears questions such as, 'Do "fresh expressions" make the message clearer or do they water it down, obscure it?' and 'If we take the word "sin" out of the baptism liturgy do we obscure the significance of the sacrament?' or 'Do "all-singing, all-dancing" Christian ministers make the divine message more accessible or do they distract the congregation from the message to the messenger?'

There is a place for drawing the attention of a congregation with something ear or eye catching; a place for humour, anecdote and illustration, though it can distract or obscure the message. Does 'Church-speak' or 'God-speak' make the Christian message seem anachronistic, cultic or outdated? Even language without any religious connotation can obscure the message. There is a story of a preacher who was thanked for his sermon by a member of his congregation. She remarked that she had enjoyed his little story about the pair o' ducks. They had reminded her of growing up on a farm, but she had to confess she was so distracted by the story of the pair o' ducks that she didn't hear the rest of the sermon and couldn't say what it was about. The preacher smiled and said nothing, especially as he had not mentioned ducks in his sermon at all. Later in the day he recalled referring to 'a paradox'!

Wrestling with the 'pair o' ducks' within us

St Paul in Romans 7:15 describes how he wrestles with the conflict within him. It is a conflict between doing the things he should do and doing the things he should not do. Do we not all wrestle with that? Paul distinguishes the good things as being of the Holy Spirit and the bad things as being of his flesh: his unredeemed nature. We may want to distinguish them differently. So before we move on to explore further the things that we wish we or others did or did not do in the name of God and his Church (self-serving ambition), let us reflect a little on what motivates us to do the right things: those things which please and honour God and lean into his ambition.

Altruism

Doing things purely to honour God and to lean wholeheartedly into God's ambitions implies total selflessness: the ultimate altruism. St Paul in his description of how love behaves (1 Corinthians 13) asserts that love is never selfish. What he is describing is pure love. Pure love is never selfish. Human love always contains at least a trace of self-interest. Only God loves perfectly, therefore only God is totally selfless. Yet we might hold that God created us out of love, yes, but out of a need to be loved back. As we have observed before, love cannot operate effectively without reciprocation. Does that suggest that God, who is Love, is not entirely altruistic? If we can bear to entertain that thought for a moment, does it bring a little comfort to our appraisal of the quality of our loving, our altruistic endeavours or our aspirations to love more perfectly?

Authorities in the field of human behaviour assert that altruism – actions of selflessness, or pro-social behaviours (as they are sometimes called) – is part of the human frame and has a variety of deeper motivations. We may perform an act of selflessness out of a deep and unconscious drive to save another. We hear of someone diving into an icy pond to rescue someone, for example. It is instinctive. Perhaps the reader, like me, has benefited from or witnessed acts of kindness, gestures of generosity and selflessness. But it may be that sometimes we are kind to others in the hope that they will be kind to us. Sometimes we behave in a kindly and altruistic way out of guilt or peer pressure. We may be motivated by duty, obligation or the prospect of reward. It may be that we are kind to others because it reinforces our view of ourselves as kind people. If someone is upset we want to comfort them. Selflessly we don't want to see them suffer. Less altruistically, we don't want to continue to witness their distress because it distresses us. When someone abruptly tells another to 'Stop crying at once. Blow your nose and cheer your face up,' they may be solely concerned to get someone out of an unhelpful mood which might trigger an asthma attack, or they may be irritated by their snivelling and wish to put a stop to it!

The aim here is not to condemn the co-mixture in us of altruism and selfishness so much as to accept it and to explore two points which arise from our human experience of it.

Mixed motives, great outcomes – first point

The first point is about the God-givenness of mixed motives. God delights in his children and he delights in our efforts to please him and he delights in our delight. What delights us motivates us; and motivation is a key factor in sustaining a work begun. So, God speaks through our sense of duty; through our wholesome desires and through the things that delight us.

There is nothing wrong with doing things because they give us a buzz. It is so much harder to do things that give us no pleasure, even though we know they have to be done! There is nothing wrong with needing to feel a sense of satisfaction or fulfilment for a job well done or well received. It can inspire us to do greater things or it can sustain us when we are less certain of the direction of our lives.

The opposite is also true. When we feel continual dissatisfaction or have little or no sense of fulfilment, we can become demotivated and demoralised. In that state we are of less use to God and his kingdom purposes.

The experience of secular organisations

Once again we could take some encouragement from secular life. It is in a company's interest to ensure that employees have some sense of job satisfaction, some sense of achievement and of appreciation. The motivation for this will not be purely pastoral. A happy and fulfilled workforce is likely to be more productive. There will be a slower turnover in the workforce (with all the saving of expense implicit in that), and sickness and absence rates will be lower. Moreover, many secular organisations have long since learned that members of the workforce work better, achieve more, stay healthier and live more happily if their efforts are appreciated, recognised and celebrated. To do so takes nothing away from the works and, generally, does not make employees morph into megalomaniacs!

Jesus understood the need to keep his disciples motivated. The mountain-top transfiguration experience for Peter, James and John is one example. It gave them a boost in morale before they set off down the plain towards Jerusalem and to the Passion of Christ. God knows our needs, and they include our very human need to be appreciated, encouraged and cherished. We, in turn, desire to please God and to show our appreciation for all he has done for us.

Mixed motives, great outcomes – second point

A second point regarding the co-mixture of altruism and selfishness in us is about degree. We might ponder to what extent our selfishness inhibits the bringing in of the kingdom. We may wonder where the boundary lies between our human need for personal fulfilment and our sinful, self-serving ambition. It is, of course, a very difficult judgement to make: whether that be in regard to ourselves or in regard to other people. Generally, it is not wise to judge others at all and hazardous to judge ourselves too harshly! There is, however, a line that is crossed where a little bit of self-centred quiet satisfaction slips into scandalous self-serving ambition. Perhaps the story of Father Cedric might serve to make this point.

Father Cedric had an appreciation of art, colour and beauty. After many years in one particular parish he was sent by his bishop to another parish. He wasn't very happy about the move but was obliged to go out of obedience. Consequently he arrived in the new parish in a bad mood. He took one look at the interior of the church and decided that the colours used on the walls were grossly offensive. Without consulting the parish, his first task was to engage decorators to repaint the entire interior of the church in colours he deemed more appropriate. His congregation, schooled in the tradition of 'what Father says, goes', said nothing – at least, not to him, though they had lots to say down at the church social club! Estimates of how much money had been spent on the redecoration varied considerably, and the figure grew exponentially with the spread of rumour on the subject. In short, the congregation was scandalised.

Once the redecoration was complete, Father Cedric condemned as 'in poor taste' several of the religious artefacts that had adorned the church for more than 150 years! He bought new ones, again without consultation. The scandalisation grew, and added to this was a deep sense of hurt and distress at the loss of the artefacts that had been the focus for devotion for so many years.

Father Cedric was deeply satisfied with what he had achieved. He was sure God would be too! He was sure, also, that in time, his parishioners would appreciate the 'improvements'. The size of the congregation remained the same as ever. No harm done.

Father Cedric's leadership style might seem outrageous to us. We might, however, envy his freedom from accountability or the constraint of diocesan advisory committees and legal faculties. But if we reflect on this incident, do we detect where, how and why selfish ambition crept into the ministry of someone who had hitherto been regarded as a good and pastoral parish priest?

Pause for reflection

In what ways does the story of Father Cedric resonate with you?

Commissioning in woundedness

We shall return to self-serving ambition, but for now we hold, gently, the phenomenon of human frailty and its value in the service of the Lord in fine balance with the dangers of human frailty causing real harm. We are but clay jars and carry the treasures of God's Spirit with care (2 Corinthians 4:7). We pray that our humanity in all its woundedness and brokenness will allow God to be God in the world, and we trust in Jesus whose body was torn for us on Calvary to bring us safely through our earthly pilgrimage of loving service. We place our hope in his resurrection and in his victory over sin and death.

The apostle Peter's life and ministry has much to teach us about fragile humanity and the greatness of our calling. Let us reflect briefly on the occasion of his healing and commissioning on the beach after Jesus' resurrection from the dead (John 21:15-19). We will remember that Peter three times denied that he knew Jesus, and now Jesus gives Peter the opportunity to be reconciled in himself as well as with Jesus. John, the writer of the Gospel, cleverly links the two occasions with his reference to a charcoal fire on both the occasion of denial and the occasion of reconciliation (John 18:18; 21:9). John wants us to mentally link the two occasions, both with the 'charcoal' reference and with the account of a threefold denial and a threefold affirmation of love.

The beach barbecue scenario is the setting for the reconciliation of a penitent and a commission to feed God's flock. Remember, however, that this is a post-Calvary, post garden of resurrection encounter between Peter and Jesus. One can imagine Jesus lifting his hands in blessing of Peter, perhaps embracing him or placing his hand on Peter's arm, but see: the hands which bless, embrace and reassure are pierced. They are wounded hands. This is a commissioning in woundedness.

Remember that before he commissioned his disciples, Jesus showed them his hands and his side. He showed them his woundedness. Then he breathed on them and said to them, 'Receive the Holy Spirit. If you forgive the sins of any, they are forgiven them; if you retain the sins of any, they are retained' (John 20:21-23). It is an awesome responsibility vested in ordinary human beings. But it was, and is, a commission in woundedness: it is carried out in a spirit of knowing one's own woundedness and unworthiness.

When sins are confessed and absolution is given, what takes place is an encounter with a penitent, which is always a reminder of the priest's own shortcomings and human frailty. The effectiveness of the sacrament is reinforced precisely because the priest has their own wounds which prevent them from being judgemental, from being 'holier than thou'.

A priest, in her or his own brokenness and woundedness, models for us all the wonder of the grace of God's Holy Spirit at work in and through us, showing us that we need not be any great shakes in order to be instruments of God's healing and reconciling grace. The minister's woundedness may be apparent and allows for the woundedness of us all, but it is a woundedness that we are expected to carry with good grace.

By the same token, Christ blesses us in our woundedness. We are his hands and his feet, but they are wounded hands and wounded feet! The desire in us to live a holy life is matched by a desire in us to live another way altogether! God knows this. God knew this before he commissioned us, in the same way that he knew Peter through and through. He saw Peter at his lowest ebb, but he could see, too, all that Peter would be for him, all Peter would do for him. Christ commissions his Church in woundedness, but we have a duty of care and a responsibility not to let our woundedness fester into destructive behaviour.

Through the lens of Jesus' own temptations we explore further, in the next chapter, the consequences of serious, life-choking and self-serving ambition.

CHAPTER SIX

Power, perspective and temptation

Having explored a little how our motives for what we do are always mixed to some degree, how we all live on a spectrum somewhere between divine altruism and complete selfishness, we continue by exploring how it is that we slide so easily along that spectrum in the direction of self-serving ambition!

The first reason might be because it is quite easy to lean away from God's ambition and to lean towards our own. God does not force us. We are not slaves. God is love, and although the 'pull' of Divine Love returns us endlessly towards himself, we drive ourselves away from Love by the attractiveness of sin. If 'sin' seems too strong a word, we should remember that to put anyone or anything above God is the sin of idolatry. It is a sin we all commit!

To be fair, we do not always deliberately defy God. We are more likely to wander off, to get caught up in something. When Jesus speaks of the sheep going astray (for example, Luke 15:4, but see also Psalm 119:176), he means getting lost rather than a deliberate act of going away. Watching sheep graze, one can see how they might be tempted by a tasty bit of something in the field just to one side, and how that leads them to another tasty bit of something a little further away. Before long the sheep has wandered off. It looks up and finds it is a long way away from where it was. It is 'lost'. For the most part, human beings are much the same.

A second reason why it is easy to put our own ambitions before those of God might be that we are very good at telling ourselves that we are doing our laudable and worthy activities because that is what God wants of us. However, in reality, the association with what God wants is difficult to identify and the activity difficult to justify. A routine question for us as we go about God's business in the Church is, 'How does what I am doing now lean into God's ambition?' Put another way, 'How is Love served by what I am now doing or saying, or not doing, not saying?' It is not a question we can dwell on continually: if we are not careful we could spend so much time asking the question that we get nothing done at all! Just occasionally it is worth stepping outside of ourselves however, outside of a situation, and asking God to enlighten us as to how what is going on honours him, pleases him, serves him. Perhaps Barbara's story might illustrate such a circumstance.

Barbara, a newly installed parish priest of a rural benefice, found herself chairing a meeting of the annual church fete committee. The committee met three times each year. At the first meeting they would review what had gone well or badly the year before. Each stallholder gave a brief (and sometimes not-so-brief) report. The weather was discussed and forecasts considered. Permissions were sought and health and safety matters raised.

At the second meeting the committee would discuss what stalls and events would be included at the upcoming fete. Barbara had listened carefully at the first meeting and had asked around prior to the second. She had learned that the fete follows the same pattern every year, with the same stallholders and event-runners doing what they had always done. She also learned that income from the fete had been gradually falling year on year. Barbara felt it was time for a few changes. She arrived at the meeting bearing an umbrella. There were ribald comments about it since the weather was fine that day, or was she anticipating a downpour at the fete? Barbara began the business of the meeting by asking the committee members to think of ways of using an umbrella apart from keeping off the rain. It was an icebreaker she had learned at college which was designed to help people to think differently, imaginatively, creatively. One or two members got the point and came up with ideas such as a water collector, a sunshade or a dibber for planting lettuces. Very quickly, however, the meeting descended into silence and awkward glances. One elderly parishioner ventured, 'I suppose we could have an umbrella stall, though we've never had one before and I can't think where we would get enough umbrellas to sell.' Barbara sank into her chair in defeat and despondency. The committee members quickly agreed that all the same stalls and events would run as in the previous year except for the 'Bash the rat' stall as poor old Mr Simpkins, who had run it for years, had died in December.

The third meeting was to discuss the beneficiaries of the proceeds of the fete which needed to be announced ahead of the event. Barbara asked the committee members to consider how best any profit might serve the gospel – the central work of the Church. Committee members represented various interests in the local church and Barbara's question shocked most of them to the core. Almost all of them had been expecting any profit to go to any one of a number of matters relating to the maintenance of the church building. The bell fund aficionado explained that the bell no longer tolled to tell the community that worship was being offered or that war was imminent. Others explained that without a new boiler the cold church would not attract worshippers (or the more lucrative weddings). Still others wanted locks to be fitted to various ancillary areas of the church so that the body of the church could be left open more often during the day for private prayer or reflection. One member wanted the funds to go towards repair of the church path which, he argued, was in such a bad state of repair that someone could fall and might sue the church for a small fortune.

Barbara ventured the idea that some of the funds could go to a local charity or to a diocesan-linked mission in Africa. The statement, 'Charity begins at home, Barbara,' spoken boldly by one parishioner, put paid to any further discussion. The funds would go to the church 'fabric fund'. Asking public opinion on the matter at the fete that summer, Barbara gathered that the local community supported the fete *only because* the proceeds went to the fabric of the church. It was felt that, as a local resource, it was important to people even if they never darkened its door. Barbara would hear many stories of those who had found comfort within its walls when no one was about or how the bell that once tolled had reminded them that God is in his heaven and all is well with the world. Barbara's ambition for a more adventurous fete did not accord with local sentiments of familiarity and reliability ('I always get my chutney at the summer fete'). Her ambitions of a congregation whose commitment to announcing the kingdom of God (by her own definition) or for improving the lives of people thousands of miles away would be met with inertia or resistance. Just occasionally she would come across parishioners who were indeed doing a lot for charities at home and abroad, but not through the auspices of the local church. She would meet others who quietly served their neighbour in a thousand ways and parishioners who quietly witnessed to the gospel in word and action. Barbara would discover, too, that God had been ahead of her, and for quite some time!

Pause for reflection

How does the annual church fete in Barbara's parish lean into God's ambitions? Put another way, how is Love served by what the fete committee members are doing?

Self-serving ambition and power

Sliding along the spectrum between divine altruism in the direction of self-serving ambition is a temptation 'oiled' by access to power. Sometimes power appears to be divinely bestowed. Have we not met people who claim a divine authority for telling us what we should do, what we should refrain from doing or how we should live? It is the person who is adamant that they have had a 'word from the Lord' that tells us to desist from this or that. They may well have had such a word! Sometimes, however, their motives are less than pure. The New Testament Church had similar problems with identifying the authenticity of 'words' of this kind. The following passage might serve as an example:

> But false prophets also arose among the people, just as there will be false teachers among you, who will secretly bring in destructive opinions. They will even deny the Master who bought them – bringing swift destruction on themselves. Even so, many will follow their licentious ways, and because of these teachers the way of truth will be maligned. And in their greed they will exploit you with deceptive words.
>
> *2 Peter 2:1-3a*

The New Testament Church quickly recognised the need to seek affirmation of a word (of prophecy) from among other members of the community (see, for example, 1 Corinthians

14:29-33). We shall reflect more on accountability in the final chapter, but for the purposes of this reflection we focus on the temptation to misuse power.

Power comes in many forms. We have touched very briefly on the power of authority but we recognise, too, the power of influence: the ability to persuade and encourage others to a course of action. Misuse of such power can so easily lead to manipulation.

We also recognise the power of expertise. When we call in a qualified and experienced craftsman to rescue us in a crisis, we are glad of their power of expertise, but such power can be misused in the way of exploitation of our ignorance or vulnerability.

There is, too, the power of information. When it is misused we can be disempowered or disenfranchised. Here the danger comes from those who would take advantage of us. There is, however, the power of disclosure: the open and honest admission of ignorance, inexperience, vulnerability or need. And there is the power of silence: the withholding of information, of permission, of absolution. This is another potent power made deadly in the wrong hands. How great is the power of authority, influence, expertise, information and disclosure when it is used to defend the weak, set free the oppressed, bring food to the hungry, or for justice and peace! Such greatness is the power of Love at work!

Power, at its best, is the awareness that one has the ability to change the lives of others for the better. Having the resources that power brings is not enough. Many might have resources but fail to appreciate that they have the power to improve someone's life with those resources. Take, for instance, the person of modest means who is persuaded by a radio advertisement that they can restore the sight of ten people in the developing world by making a very modest donation to a certain charity. That is power, both the power of advertising and the power of giving.

The temptations of Christ

It would seem remiss to reflect on the temptation to misuse power without reference to the temptations Jesus encountered in the desert at the beginning of his ministry.

> Jesus, full of the Holy Spirit, returned from the Jordan and was led by the Spirit in the wilderness, where for forty days he was tempted by the devil. He ate nothing at all during those days, and when they were over, he was famished.
>
> *Luke 4:1, 2*

The temptation narratives appear in all three synoptic Gospels (Matthew, Mark and Luke), though Mark says very little. Matthew's and Luke's accounts are very similar in describing three of what we might imagine were just a few of the temptations Jesus faced. From the narratives it is clear that it was a time for Jesus to consider his power: his ability to challenge, to change, to rescue and to renew. It was the beginning of Jesus' ministry and a time of transition in his life, and it was a time of trial and a time of testing. A brief reflection on each of the three recorded temptations might help us to consider temptation in contemporary Church life.

First temptation:
stones into bread

In the first of the three 'temptations of Christ', we are told that the period of fasting for 40 days and 40 nights was over when 'the tempter' approached Jesus and said, 'If you are the Son of God, command these stones to become loaves of bread.' Jesus quoted the Scriptures, trumping the tempter's focus with the more expansive, 'One does not live by bread alone, but by every word that comes from the mouth of God' (Matthew 4:3, 4). We note that it would be a word rather than an action of Jesus that would change the stones into bread, and that Jesus' reply is about words that come from the mouth of God. Words rather than actions seem to characterise this encounter.

There are those who, by their words, can change things. At its most altruistic and evangelistic we may cite great evangelists like Billy Graham whose power of oratory drew vast crowds to repentance and to commitment to Christ. He would argue, however, that it is Christ who calls and that it is the power of the Holy Spirit that changes people's lives, but we recognise the power of oratory to be the vehicle of God-given change. In the same way, we recognise the power of oratory communicated through the media, bringing to our attention the plight of the hungry in hard-hitting appeals for aid. The hard 'stones' of shocking and confronting oratory can bring bread to those with nothing to eat.

By contrast, we might cite Adolf Hitler, whose undoubted power of oratory changed the shape of Europe and beyond, and brought about the suffering and death of millions of people. Here we understand that it is the source of the oration that makes the difference. It is 'every word that comes from the mouth of *God*', and not any of the words that come from the evil intrinsic in the powers of self-serving ambition.

The preached 'word' is of great importance to Church life. Some say it is more important than anything else, and great emphasis is put upon it in acts of worship. Since the

Reformation, the architecture of churches built in each generation tells us how this is so. The size, height and placing of a pulpit gives us a clue as to the prominence given to preaching.

Pulpits apart (and many don't use one at all!), preachers are something else. Classes for those training to be preachers will vary according to the tradition of the institution offering the training, but they will cover such areas as biblical exegesis, exposition, interpretation, illustration and delivery. These are the 'stock in trade' of the preacher. Yet standing before the congregation with the intention to preach is a human being. Readers experienced in listening to sermons will have spotted those occasions when the preacher treats the congregation as their therapist and the pulpit as the 'couch' on which to pour out their woes. Then there are those who offer tirades against church authority, bishops, academics – indeed, any individual or group that the preacher has a particular problem with at any given time. The reader may know the old expression 'six feet above contradiction'? It takes a brave member of a congregation to challenge a preacher about their sermon. It is harder still when the preacher claims they were guided by the Holy Spirit in their preparation! A preacher who is never open to criticism may become more and more self-deluded. They may not be aware of their shortcomings but, conversely, a preacher who never gets feedback may never know just how well they preach! Self-delusion can lead to low self-esteem and this may adversely affect the quality of the preaching.

There are times, however, when something a preacher has said has resonated deeply. It may have disturbed us, even enraged us, but it set us in a train of thought that turned the stones of our resistance into malleable 'dough' which God then formed into 'bread' for the world. Sometimes a preacher, thanked for inspiring us so, will reply that the sermon had been dashed off minutes before the service or that they, themselves, thought it the worst sermon they had ever preached! Somehow, in spite of self-serving oration and downright wicked intent on the part of the preacher, the Holy Spirit triumphs!

Second temptation:
the glory of the kingdoms of the world – adulation and celebrity

We read:

> Then the devil led him up and showed him in an instant all the kingdoms of the world. And the devil said to him, 'To you I will give their glory and all this authority; for it has been given over to me, and I give it to anyone I please. If you, then, will worship me, it will all be yours.'
>
> *Luke 4:5-7*

The sudden discovery that we have power (in any form) can be quite a shock. We pray we may use it wisely. Most of us rely on the accountability or checks and balances that are in place to help us to use power wisely. It is not enough to argue that we are accountable to God on the Day of Judgement: we need some accountability here and now. Such accountability is not a yoke to constrain us but simply a device to steer us away from the 'ditches' of error. Some people in Church life have much more power than they realise, and the more power they have, the more accountability is required. The following story might help to illustrate something of this.

Reverend Mother Catherine tucked the skirt of her habit under her seat and quietly closed the door of the ancient community car. She drove sedately down the drive, through the great gates of the convent and turned into the main road. Then she put her foot down on the accelerator and thundered up the hill. She followed the road round and up above the convent before pulling off the road into a lay-by. She pulled off her white bonnet, to which was attached her long black veil, and tossed it onto the passenger seat. She got out of the car and surveyed the view. Taking in a very deep breath she exhaled loudly while massaging her cropped hair and scalp as if she were shampooing it under the warm, early spring sunshine. The view was stunning.

Below lay the convent. The chapel stood at the heart of the complex of buildings. To the side of it stood the round Chapter House building where, two hours earlier, Sister Catherine, Mistress of Novices, had been elected Reverend Mother. God certainly had a sense of humour. How often had she said, 'If I were Reverend Mother I would . . .'? Now she was! She knew she now had virtually unlimited power. Advice was readily available, but she knew that she could ignore any advice given and follow her own judgement.

Mother Catherine let her eyes take in more of the convent buildings and grounds. She could see the neat rows of vegetables in the kitchen garden. The discipline of that garden was in stark contrast to the chaos of the adjacent chicken run and the rough patch of ground where the goat was tethered. Caught by the thin sunlight was the glass of the conservatory roof. The changing light gave the impression of signals being sent out, but what could they mean? This rather grand metal and glass construction had been erected during her predecessor's time and was the second such structure to be built on that spot in recent years.

Twenty years before, when Catherine was a junior sister, the then Reverend Mother had, on a whim, bought a conservatory. It was to be a warm and sunny place where ageing and infirm sisters could contemplate the garden without getting a chill. Soon after the next election, the new Reverend Mother had it pulled down, condemning it as an extravagance. Again, this was done without consulting the community.

Five years in elected office soon passes in convent life, and the then Reverend Mother, having been voted out, reluctantly vacated the chair of St Monica. Her successor's first act was to commission the present magnificent conservatory. Although, once again, there was no consultation, there was general assent. This was expressed almost wordlessly in the way that only those who live with silence can do so well.

'What will *you* do, Catherine?' a voice whispered in her ear. 'You know you can do anything you like!' The conservatory roof winked and blinked at her, and Catherine thought of the text from the reading at Matins that morning: 'the devil took him to a very high mountain and showed him all the kingdoms of the world and their splendour' (Matthew 4:8).

It was getting a little chilly. Catherine returned to the car and popped her bonnet back onto her head. She drove slowly across the ridge, down the hill and in through the convent gates. She parked the car and walked along the long path around the side of the house. She noticed Sister Paul tying wire around nails she had hammered into the orchard wall, the better to train the fronds of an early-flowering jasmine. Sister Paul's stretching revealed her leg calliper and built-up shoe. She had suffered from polio as a child and now, well into her seventies, she still needed the leg support. Mother Catherine noted that the shoe was very worn and consequently less effective. She made a note to herself to have Sister Paul seen by a specialist and to get her kitted out with something better.

Coming around the south side of the convent, Mother Catherine came upon the magnificent conservatory with its ornate wrought ironwork in the Victorian style. She let herself in through doors that opened on to the lawn, noting how the green floor-covering matched the colour of the grass outside, somehow bringing the garden inside. As she passed she was greeted by a frail, elderly nun who had been parked in her wheelchair so that she could see out of the window. 'Congratulations, Reverend Mother!' she said.

'Thank you, Sister, I think!' replied Catherine to the sister who had pulled down the first conservatory all those years ago.

Looking shyly round the conservatory, the former Mother, with a glint in her eye, said, 'I hope, dear Mother, that you won't be taking away this sacred space!'

'No', replied Reverend Mother, gently, 'I won't.' As she left the sun-filled conservatory for the cool shade of the house, she added, 'Pray for me, Sister. Pray for me.'

In all these things, and in a world that few will experience first-hand, Mother Catherine has power. One senses that she will use it well, to make a difference to the well-being of the other sisters who will look to her for everything from shoelaces to health care. There will be others to advise her if she is willing to listen. They will have the power of experience and acquired wisdom. Catherine may want to change things, as her predecessors had changed things. The ability to implement change is not the same as having the power to change. Many an organisation has foundered because vital change has been sabotaged by the inertia of a workforce resistant to such change.

Catherine is relatively unfettered in the exercise of power, but unfortunately there may be too few checks and balances to modify or squash any of her wilder ideas. Clearly Catherine recognises the awesomeness of the power to which she has been elected. She will appreciate, too, that the community of sisters would not have elected her to high office if they thought she could not do the job. Those elected to high office have been known to surprise everyone once the 'mitre' has been placed on the brow! In recent history we have seen the election of Pope John XXIII. Apparently appointed as a safe pair of hands until a more suitable candidate emerged, Pope John brought change to the Roman Catholic Church in a way no one could have imagined: change which most of Christendom has applauded.

The temptation of fame

Adulation and celebrity profile might sound like modern-day phenomena, but our history books will tell us of those who have stood out and been feted and carried shoulder-high. It is not always clear whether such people courted that or welcomed it. Mark's story might aid our reflections.

Mark had been ordained for some years and had ministered in a number of locations before becoming parish priest of a large market-town church. He viewed his successful application for the post as 'promotion' – or, in church-speak, 'preferment' – as a reward for his hard work in some very tough inner-city areas. He had twice been physically assaulted and had even made the newspaper headlines under the title 'Vicar turns the other cheek'. He had lost count of the number of times he had been verbally abused. Mark had grown in strength and confidence as each challenge had been met successfully. The problem was that he now considered himself invincible: that no challenge was beyond him. He hadn't reckoned on the congregation at St Stephen's!

Within weeks of arriving in the parish he had been reported to the bishop for giving out 'aggressive notices' and for courting local newspaper headlines by speaking out unguardedly about church business. He was advised to try less hard, and to 'plane with the grain' rather than across it – a carpentry metaphor that was completely lost on him. Mark was determined that when he came to leave St Stephen's he would leave behind him a legacy of his ministry. He hoped, one day, to be famous for all he had achieved. After he had gone he would be remembered. He was sure of that.

One day, seemingly alone in the church, he wandered around looking at the monuments and plaques that cluttered the walls. 'I'll have those out,' he thought aloud.

'No you won't,' said a voice behind him.

Startled, and ready to defend himself, Mark turned to find an elderly woman sitting in a pew and partially hidden behind a pillar. 'And you are?' said Mark.

The woman got up and introduced herself. She was a visitor. She had come to the church because her grandfather had been vicar there and she wanted to remind herself of him and of the place where she used to swing on the communion rail and squeal with delight. She led Mark to a board at the back of the church. In gold letters was a list of the priests who had served at St Stephen's from Aelred of Bec in the fourteenth century to the present day. She pointed to her grandfather's name. Mark's name was the last on the long list, the gold of the letters brighter than all the rest.

The woman explained that the plaque on the wall (the one which Mark had been looking at when he made his remark) and the entry of her grandfather's name on the board at the back of the church were the only public evidence that he had served there. She went on to point out a few of the names from former centuries and to relate to Mark why they had been famous or infamous. She placed her hand gently on Mark's arm. 'Sir,' the woman addressed him (not knowing quite how he preferred to be addressed), 'which

will you be: famous or infamous?' Without waiting for a
reply she continued, 'I suspect you will be neither but that
you will be one of this long list of faithful clergy who have
done what they could and put up with plenty, but whose
deeds, for the most part, are now known only to God who
will have rewarded them appropriately.' Then she turned
and left the church.

Mark did not leave for some time, well after darkness had
descended. Once he had stopped protesting and cursing the
cheek of the old woman, and after he had ranted at God
in self-justification, he cried and sobbed and prayed a little
before he went home chastened and reflective.

Third temptation:
invincibility

In the Holy Scriptures we read, 'Then the devil took him to
Jerusalem, and placed him on the pinnacle of the temple,
saying to him, "If you are the Son of God, throw yourself
down from here"' (Luke 4:9).

Scholars differ on how much Jesus knew about his own
identity and whether that identity was revealed to him
from the beginning of his earthly life or later – perhaps
when he was baptised by John in the Jordan. Wherever and
whenever it was, Jesus discovered the answer to the eternal
question, 'Who am I?' He came to know that he is God. It
would seem that it wasn't an easy thing to come to terms
with! If it was difficult for Jesus, then it is likely to be very
difficult for us to come to terms with the loftiness of our
own calling. If we are called to let God in Christ come into
our lives and to take us over, then we shall become like
Christ; we shall become one with God, indistinguishable
in every way.

If Jesus has discovered this about himself then perhaps he could have flown off the parapet of the Temple, had it not been for one thing: Jesus has also discovered human constraint. For God to come to earth in any meaningful way he would have to live within the constraints of being human. Sadly, this human flesh is earthbound and does not fly without mechanical aid. We are fragile earth-beings who plummet disastrously to the ground unless we are wearing a parachute!

Jesus, propelled into the desert by the Holy Spirit, is confronted with self-knowledge. That confrontation, in the form of temptations by the devil, includes the issues of invincibility and vulnerability implicit in the temptation to throw himself off the parapet of the Temple. Sometimes we come willingly before God with questions of self-knowledge, and sometimes life circumstances force that upon us.

The Holy Spirit who has propelled Jesus into the desert enables him to commune with the Father and provides him with a necessary 'space' in which to reflect on what he needs to do next. Following his desert experience, Jesus is drawn back into the melee of human life. Both Matthew and Mark link the end of the desert experience with the exit of John the Baptist from the scene (John having been arrested). We recall the words of John: 'He must increase, but I must decrease' (John 3:30).

Jesus, filled with the message brought by the prophets, and latterly by John the Baptist, takes up the call to repentance because the kingdom of heaven had come upon earth. Jesus, the embodiment of that kingdom, is come upon earth and he is ready, willing and able to see the fulfilment of his destiny and that of all God's people. Luke describes Jesus as 'filled with the power of the Spirit' (Luke 4:14) and has Jesus striding through Galilee and laying down his credentials with great boldness in the synagogue of his home town of Nazareth.

We reflected earlier on the passage of Holy Scripture from which Jesus read in the synagogue. Then we were reflecting on vocation. Here we consider his actions in relation to his self-discovery of power – the power to change people's lives for the better. The passage is worthy of further reflection:

> The Spirit of the Lord is upon me,
> because he has anointed me
> to bring good news to the poor.
> He has sent me to proclaim release to the captives
> and recovery of sight to the blind,
> to let the oppressed go free,
> to proclaim the year of the Lord's favour.
>
> *Luke 4:18-21, citing Isaiah 61:1-3*

'Today,' he declares, 'this scripture has been fulfilled in your hearing.'

Having been propelled into the desert, Jesus re-emerges at the end of one experience and at the threshold of another. It appears that during that time he has come to know more clearly what he is capable of doing and what he needs to do. We are capable of doing many things (many of them entirely unacceptable to God!), but discerning what we *need* to do is something that requires regular reappraisal.

Power and self-awareness

As we consider who we are and what we are capable of doing, we view possibilities through the lens of our understanding of God's ambition. We appraise them, too, through acknowledging not only our gifts but also the opportunities we have to exercise them. Such reflection is set against a degree of self-knowledge and self-awareness. We know our temptation areas, our weaknesses, the ways we can so easily misuse power. Mark's encounter with the elderly woman caused him to reappraise his ministerial style and his personal goals. That encounter led him to meet with an experienced priest who became a spiritual director and mentor to him for the whole of his time at St Stephen's. He was able to deepen his self-awareness and self-knowledge by making a 30-day retreat accompanied by an experienced guide, but not before he had experienced shorter periods of guided solitude and reflection.

Deepening self-awareness requires a degree of introspection. However, too much introspection can render us hyper-scrupulous and self-absorbed. Too little introspection might mean that we do not notice that we have changed or that we have gained a different perspective on life. Even if we do not think *we* have changed, the context in which we live might have changed, and that may change how we live in terms of maturity, of wisdom and of learning from our mistakes. We learn from our mistakes, and also from our triumphs. This is just as important because what we have managed to do well for God once might be done again.

All these aspects are about self-knowledge – and more: they are about our growing identity in Christ. Remember that St Paul, with all his faults and his history of the persecution of Christians, could cry, 'It is no longer I who live, but it is Christ who lives in me' (Galatians 2:20). I know of a fine priest who has had those words embroidered on the *inside* of his ordination stole so that every time he puts on his stole he is reminded of his true identity.

Pause for reflection

If Jesus were to offer himself for selection for ordained ministry, declaring who he believes he is and the power and authority given to him by the Father, would he be recommended for training?

Power and servanthood

In the desert, Jesus is taunted by the devil to misuse his power. Jesus, freshly empowered by the Holy Spirit, discovers his identity and the power that goes with it. Jesus would be aware of the way earthly kings use their power. He knows, too, that as King of heaven and earth, he has the power to overrule all power, but he realises that this is not the way to go. Jesus must lay aside all earthly power and become a servant (Philippians 2:5-8).

The paradox of power and powerlessness comes together in the mystery of the cross. Stripped of power, Jesus is abused, taunted, tortured and killed. Yet what looks like a victory for the powers of evil is turned into a glorious victory for the King of heaven and earth, the legacy of which we shall enjoy for ever. The wonder of the Lord's death and rising is in the exercise of supreme servanthood, but without the slightest loss of majesty.

We left the story of Mother Catherine as she parted from the elderly wheelchair-bound nun in the conservatory. What was that glint in the elderly sister's eye all about? The reader may recall that she had been the one to pull down the previous conservatory because she thought it was an extravagance. Now she refers to the new conservatory as 'sacred space'. In her mellowed old age and infirmity she has come to treasure a sun-filled, wind-free spot in which to pray and reflect on the goodness and generosity of God. When she held the powerful position of Reverend Mother she may have done many good things, and it would be very sad if she were to be remembered only for the destruction of the old conservatory. She is relatively powerless now, and dependent on others for nearly everything, and yet one senses that she is at peace with herself. She is not exploited or abused but cared for and cherished. Having very little power may not, of itself, be a problem. It is the exploitation of vulnerability and powerlessness that is an outrage. She has known both power and powerlessness. Do we?

When we exercise any power that affects the lives of others, we are accountable to God for it. All power belongs to him, and any power we have is delegated power. We know, too, that in our powerlessness, God will not abuse us or exploit us. We can rest in him who is our 'sacred space' and allow him to serve our needs. As loyal servants of God, we serve others by the power of God and we let Christ the Servant King serve us and serve others through us.

Power and vulnerability

I am sure we have all discovered our vulnerability, but knowing of our vulnerabilities and coping with them may be a different matter. We might have learned something of how to live with our vulnerability and of how to prevent ourselves from being too hurt too often by what happens to us. We might have learned a little of how to prevent ourselves becoming victims of our vulnerability, how to self-talk our way out of low self-esteem, but it may be only when we are faced with a major life crisis that these things are really tested.

We have learned that it was in this very vulnerability that Jesus would save the world. In his death on the cross, and in his being raised from death by the Father, God would fuse vulnerability and invincibility together in a spectacular way. The outcome was glorious; nothing less than triumph for God and new life for us vulnerable mortals en route to the Godhead.

From what follows in the Gospel accounts, it is clear that the 40 days in the desert were formative for Jesus. He emerged triumphant in the face of temptation: triumphant but not triumphalist. He knows, and takes seriously, the human temptation to self-serving ambition. In his compassion, he recognises that altruism and selfishness coexist. He discovered invincibility tempered by human constraint. Problems occur when we lose sight of that paradox. We hear the mantra, 'You can do anything you want to do, be anything you want to be.' But is that true? Could all be brain surgeons if they wanted to be? Do all have the opportunities of education, financial security or friends in high places? Clearly not. For example, not everyone is going to be a great sculptor like Michaelangelo but one never knows where the next great sculptor will come from! God does do extraordinary things through ordinary human beings, but there is a balance to be struck, an awareness of potential in relation to reality. We are not invincible.

What, then, makes for a sense of invincibility? What happens when pipe dreams become nightmares? It is only when we try to live without grace, when we delude ourselves into thinking we can do anything we like – and all on our own – that we slide disastrously so far along the spectrum in the direction of selfishness that we collapse, sometimes taking others down with us. Much of self-serving ambition is rooted in wilfulness, stubbornness and pride, for which the antidote is prayer of repentance and the humility to ask for God's help.

There is a phenomenon that produces selfish ambition, both in the Church and in secular society, which has its roots in a psychopathological disorder we used to call 'megalomania' but which nowadays goes by the name of 'narcissism'. Its impact on the Church is the subject of the next chapter.

CHAPTER SEVEN

Distorting the image and likeness of God

Behind the mask

Jesus is God unmasked. He shows us the Father and reveals his love for us.

When we speak of people wearing 'masks', we might suppose they wear them to hide their identity or to disguise their unattractiveness. Perhaps the opposite is also sometimes true. We put on masks to give ourselves permission to behave in unattractive ways, masking from the world the God-given beauty within us.

Sometimes we are allowed glimpses behind the masks that people wear. It is like a sunbeam appearing and disappearing from behind a dark cloud. We are treated to glimpses of God. Some people wear their masks so seldom that we regularly see God's face in theirs. They dazzle us with God's beauty! We are tempted to ask them to wear a veil, like Moses did when he came down the mountain, his face shining as a result of his encounter with God (Exodus 34:29-35). Which is the truth: that we are sunlight masked by clouds of sin and disobedience, or that we are darkness masquerading as light? According to the Book of Genesis we were created in the image and likeness of God (Genesis 1:26). Sin and disobedience have marred that image – or at least, that image has been obscured by masks, one of which is named 'self-centredness'. By God's grace those masks are peeled from us, but we snap them back into place so easily, so quickly!

One could imagine that if a 'mask' of self-serving ambition were to be worn continuously, we would become so used to wearing it that it would become part of us and it would have a damaging effect on the deeper 'tissues' of our being. There would be damage that would be difficult to repair.

In this chapter we continue to reflect on the nature and impact within the Church of self-serving ambition. We have acknowledged that our motives are always mixed to some degree, and we have begun to explore what happens when ambition begins to slip towards the self-serving end of the spectrum. We have acknowledged selfishness as sin, but here we ask ourselves whether some self-centredness might be pathological, whether it requires treatment rather than admonition. Perhaps the 'mask' of self-serving ambition is actually 'scar tissue': the image and likeness of God marred by psychopathological disorder.

Also, as we continue to make the link between vocation and ambition, we ask ourselves what part personality traits play and whether or not some personality types are more or less prone to self-centredness and self-aggrandisement. Clearly it is our experience that flattery, for example, is received by people in different ways. Some will be embarrassed by it; some will be distrustful of it while others will lap it up or, indeed, court it. Flattery may not be a very helpful thing, but sincere praise and appreciation is. Some people will be built up in confidence by it and encouraged by it, and may well extend their skills and competencies, thus making a greater contribution to God's mission in the world. So often one hears stories of people not being praised (sincerely or otherwise!) or not being appreciated, and although there may not be so many stories of being deliberately denigrated or belittled, stories abound of the demoralisation that results from receiving no positive feedback.

One hears, too, of people in leadership roles in the Church who are insecure in themselves and who feel threatened by others, such as those who are more experienced, better educated or better qualified than themselves. Some threats are entirely illusory or else cannot be weighed in any objective manner, such as those who feel threatened by those they consider to be more holy than they! A bishop once commented to me about a colleague, 'He is the only priest in the diocese who feels threatened by a compliment!' Insecurity and threat come out in conversations about how others seem to get attractive or prestigious posts. Envy is an issue, but so is the sense of having been overlooked. Sometimes people have been overlooked and one wonders why! Sometimes people who are in a position to offer someone a role that would utilise their gifts and experience appear not to do so because the candidate might be a threat, lest they 'come too near the throne'!

With so many good candidates chasing relatively few 'senior' positions, it is likely that some very able people will be disappointed. This may lead to frustration and a lowering of morale, with all the potential debilitation that can bring.

Stories abound of clergy behaving badly, and opinion is divided on whether instances of bad behaviour are more prevalent inside the Church than beyond it. Whatever the scale of it, the scandal it brings is unedifying. Responses to such behaviour are also mixed. There are those who want always to excuse it (which is not necessarily the same as to forgive it), while others take a punitive approach with seemingly no compassion or pastoral care, not only for the perpetrator but also for the victims and others caught up in the situation. To be fair, not all bad behaviour happens in an open and obvious way, and it can take years for it to be recognised, for victims to feel able to come forward or for crimes to be exposed. So often it is difficult to discern whether behaviour is born out of badness, sadness or madness, or a combination of all three: mask upon mask upon mask.

This reflection has to have some parameters, and so we might find it closer to the purpose of the book to reflect on the less obvious ways in which self-serving ambition is given rein through the force of personality, whether psychopathologically based or not. We rely not only on any psychological or sociological expertise of our own, but also on what we have observed or experienced or recognise in ourselves. Here is a short story to illustrate the impact of personality on the missional life of the Church.

Steven, a dynamic, entrepreneurial and somewhat gumptious priest, approached a diocesan committee for funding to set up a parish-based 'outreach' project – an internet café. He bounced into the interview with an electronic presentation and a short video recording which mostly featured himself in various poses of pastoral helpfulness. His smile never faltered once as he 'sold' his idea to the slightly bewildered panel. His financial information and business plan were laid out impressively in colour-coded spreadsheets. His delivery was 'awesome', or so he told his colleagues afterwards.

On the same afternoon, Jacqueline, a dedicated priest with flare and imagination who served in another part of the same diocese, tabled a very similar project. She was a little nervous but clear in her own mind that the project was something that would make a difference to the people in her parish. Her team had prayed about the project and thought about it from every angle for nearly two years. Her financial projections and business plan were well worked out and modestly presented. Jacqueline was asking for the same amount of money to set up the project as had Steven.

The committee, with limited funds to offer, decided to award the money to Steven. They saw that both projects were comparable but they were so impressed with Steven's energy and enthusiasm and the trouble to which he had gone to prepare for the presentation. Jacqueline went away sad but determined and, with the help of her congregation, found the necessary funds to set up the internet café. Steven was delighted but not surprised, since he had been so awesome on the day.

Jacqueline's church project went from strength to strength. Steven's folded within six months because he would not let anyone but himself control and manage it and because he couldn't find sufficient volunteers to work in it. Indeed, Steven spent so much time on the project that he neglected his other pastoral duties and his congregation began to desire that he would move on.

Pause for reflection

What has been your experience of the power of personality in relation to vocation and ambition?

Attractiveness and self-serving ambition

A read through the Gospels with the 12 disciples of Jesus in mind will give us thumbnail sketches of a motley crew of men who were as human as we are in every way. Indeed, there is nothing to attract our attention to them! They fight and squabble; they moan and groan; they fail, regularly, to understand. We might well ask why Jesus chose them! Reading through the rest of the New Testament, we hear something of how they turned out.

We reflected in an earlier chapter on the fate of James and John. Their fate was shared by all the rest, including the disillusioned Judas Iscariot. Christian discipleship is costly. If Jesus had chosen 12 paragons of virtue, fine men (or women) of impeccable character, all of them a bit like the Old Testament David ('Now he was ruddy, and had beautiful eyes, and was handsome' (1 Samuel 16:12b)), we may have found it impossible to emulate them. The fact that they are like us and that they, by the power of the Holy Spirit, could do such great things for God makes it possible for us to contemplate becoming disciples ourselves.

Unfortunately, in today's Western culture, attractiveness is important. One has only to see how senior politicians change in appearance as stylists and media aficionados advise on image and presentation. The drive to become 'ruddy' and 'handsome' is big business. We recognise, however, that when we meet true beauty in someone it has little to do with height or complexion. The clue to how to behold true beauty is in that same passage from the first Book of Samuel:

> When they came, [Samuel] looked on Eliab and thought, 'Surely the Lord's anointed is now before the Lord.' But the Lord said to Samuel, 'Do not look on his appearance or on the height of his stature, because I have rejected him; for the Lord does not see as mortals see; they look on the outward appearance, but the Lord looks on the heart.'
>
> *1 Samuel 16:6, 7*

The question on which we might reflect is whether or not we are swayed by attractiveness when it comes to the selection or appointment of leaders in the Church. Do we discern the inner beauty of the presence of Christ in someone regardless of outward appearance? Does charm blind us to faults which may lead to behaviours that will have devastating consequences for God's people? Certainly, personality has a bearing on discernment and decision making, but it is not always easy to recognise what combination of personality, circumstance and occurrence provides a climate in which self-serving ambition can have full rein. For example, we need risk-takers – people who will be prepared to try something out or lead the flock into pastures new. However, risk-taking can lead to an Icarus-like catastrophe without some checks and balances, some accountability. We need charismatic[6] people who can inspire us but who will not bully us or overwhelm us.

An instance of this can be found in Hugo who, as we noted earlier, is assertive and has a charm that makes him a little less irritating than he might have been. There is a fine boundary, however, between a charm offensive and an offensive charm, and Hugo has begun to make regular skirmishes across the border. He has become less inclined to use charm to forward a selfless project and more inclined to use it for the purposes of self-focus. When someone brings so much to their ministry which is positive, good and creative (as indeed Hugo has done), we might be more inclined to overlook their shortcomings. Unfortunately, the slide towards self-serving ambition can be quite insidious, rendering unjustifiable people's former appreciation of our achievements and their loyalty towards us.

Sensitivity, timing, explanation and judgement are essential for bringing people along with us. For example, we need people who are able to use all the tools of modern communication in the service of the gospel, but not to terrify the technophobes! It is a mistake to imagine that one leadership style suits all situations. When the church building catches fire in the

---

[6] The word 'charismatic' is used here in its broader secular sense rather than in relation to the charism of the Holy Spirit.

middle of Sunday worship, a calm but directive style is called for. There is no time to consult, to set up a working party or the like. When it comes to the redecoration of the vestry or sacristy, however, a different leadership style is required: one which is predicated on patience and time so that agreement can be reached over colours and finishes. Remember Father Cedric!

We might subscribe to the view that God calls all personality types to leadership roles in his Church. However true that is, it is not the same as holding that they are to have free, unbridled rein. All are accountable not only to God, but also to the people of God who have called them in God's name for their ministries. This is something to ponder on in the final chapter, but for this reflection we consider how to check the infiltration of the cult of personality while celebrating the rich diversity of personalities through whom God is doing great things. It is the reality check of personality in the service of God as distinct from the fantasy of 'personality' as the word is used in relation to a culture of 'celebrity'.

'Ya gotta get real'

We left the Conference Four taking a break from the business of the 'Going for God' conference. Having enjoyed their dinner and their break, they reassembled to hear a keynote speaker. The gist of the address was to encourage the audience to 'get real' and to 'keep it real'. Getting 'it' and keeping 'it' was unpacked as the need to appreciate how the world is, what its needs are and what the Church should be doing about it. The speaker wanted to close the gap between fantasy and reality, the way, as a Church, we hold on too much to our idiosyncratic ways, our out-of-date language and what was referred to as 'bad theology'.

Derek nodded off during the session but woke up from time to time, especially when the speaker shouted down the microphone, 'Ya gotta get real!', which was something that occurred on a number of occasions. When asked later what he thought of the address, Derek said he found himself thinking of the etymology of the word 'real'. He was pretty sure it came from the same root word as 'regal'. He said that tennis came to mind, or was it a small silver coin in the 1580s? Derek was too tired to think!

Keeping Church life real is about keeping it regal. Not in the way that King Canute understood himself as having the power to send back the sea, or King Charles I, who was so certain of the 'divine right of kings' that he believed himself accountable directly to God and to God alone. Keeping it regal means modelling our ministries on that of Jesus Christ, King of heaven and King of earth, by whose grace we are a royal priesthood, a holy nation, God's own people in order that we may proclaim the mighty acts of him who called us out of darkness into his marvellous light (1 Peter 2:9 paraphrased).

Keeping it real is about keeping it royal and leaning into God's royal ambition. Margery Williams in her much-loved book, *The Velveteen Rabbit*, encourages the reader to ask themselves what we mean by being real. Her central character, the toy rabbit, became real and alive because it was loved. Our loving God loves us into being fully alive. Loving God back makes God more 'real' to us. Loving God and leaning into God's ambitious love means vigilance and having the courage to check unacceptable behaviour. We look, again and again, to the image of God unmasked in Jesus and to his teaching and example. He demonstrates and models for us sacrificial leadership that is a puzzle to those who have not grasped the true nature of God's love. It is paradoxical and is to be lived out in the gentle power of the Holy Spirit. Prophecy needs testing, and love – true godly love – is the 'litmus paper'. Greg and Frank's story might illustrate something of this.

Greg and Frank

Greg had not seen his old friend Frank for more than 40 years. Greg had been best man at Frank's wedding. Soon after the event Greg had joined the army and, having been posted to a number of foreign bases, had lost contact with Frank. Greg had found Frank using a website designed to help old friends to get together. As young men they had been part of the same church youth group.

Greg's experience of combat and his encounter with people of many faiths or no faith at all had made him cynical about God but generous about difference and diversity in people's search for God. Frank had stayed faithful to the chapel that had nurtured him as a teenager and had retained much of the stance the chapel held on matters of faith and morals. Frank had become an elder of the church and was much respected by the congregation.

Frank and Greg's meeting was poignant and warm, but after the preliminary conversations about family, health and travel there was a gentle silence between them. As they talked about family, Greg remembered that Frank's father had been a staunch chapel-goer and had also been a wealthy man having worked hard for many years, first in the building trade and later as a property developer. Greg remembered that Frank's father had had a poor opinion of Frank and had constantly told him he was a 'ne'er do well'.

Frank offered to show Greg around the countryside. As they travelled they pointed out places they both knew and they commented on how much things had changed. They stopped at the top of a hill and looked down a valley. Frank said, 'God has blessed me richly. I have a lovely family and a fine house.' He told Greg how God had spoken to him and told him that he was to buy their current home. It was not so far from their previous house but it was bigger and rather splendid and set in half an acre of ground. So sure was Frank that God had spoken to him in this way that he went straight to the estate agent and made an offer and began the process of putting their current house on the market. He did this even before he spoke to his wife on the matter. Greg queried this and Frank's reply shocked him: 'Beryl knows that I am the head of the household and she vowed to obey me in all things.' Greg fell silent.

As they stared out of the windscreen of the car, Frank pointed to a large house just down the valley. 'That,' he said, 'was my father's house.' Instantly, Greg understood everything. He connected his memory of Frank's father's regular dismissal of his son's prospects with the 'word from the Lord' about the house. Frank's family home was of a style and a size comparable to that of his father's old home. In Greg's world he might have said, 'My father did not expect me to do well but I worked hard and I did. I now have a house every bit as good as my father's!'

Greg ventured, 'So you did as well as the old man in the end, eh Frank?'

Frank looked shocked. 'That has nothing to do with it. God has richly blessed my faithfulness.'

They fell silent once more. Little else was said between them before Frank drove Greg to the station. They didn't stay in touch.

Pause for reflection

What questions does the story of Greg and Frank raise?

Distorting the image and likeness: narcissism

We noted earlier that, according to the Bible, God chose to make us in his image and likeness (Genesis 1:26). We noted, also, that God's image and likeness is distorted in us. Among the reasons for that distortion is our self-centredness. To a greater or lesser extent we do not, out of generous love for God, seek his image or likeness. We do not seek it in the faces of others or indeed in our own reflection. Again, to a greater or lesser extent, we all seek, find and fall in love with our own reflection. We are all narcissists!

In Greek mythology, Narcissus (Νάρκισσος) was a hunter renowned for his beauty. He was said to be exceptionally proud, haughty and disdainful of the people around him. The god Nemesis is said to have encouraged Narcissus to look at his own reflection in a pool of water, and the story goes that Narcissus fell in love with the image he saw in the pool, not realising that it was his own reflection. There are different versions of what happened next. Some scholars suggest that he was so taken with his own reflection that he died, while others suggest he committed suicide – presumably in despair at not achieving union with the one reflected in the water with whom he had fallen hopelessly in love. Narcissus' obsession with himself gave the name to the psychological phenomenon of 'narcissism'.

Authorities in the field agree that each and every one of us has a degree of narcissism and that a significant degree of it gives rise to a psychological condition known as Narcissistic Personality Disorder. There would seem to be no demarcation to show when natural narcissism turns into a personality disorder. Some authorities find it helpful to ask a series of key questions, the answers to which give clues as to the degree of narcissism. There would seem to be no absolutely clear and definitive picture of Narcissistic Personality Disorder, but authorities tend to include the following signs and symptoms:

- lack of empathy, difficulty putting themselves in the position of another
- self-absorption, self-preoccupation
- preoccupation with self-image; excessive personal grooming
- easily 'wounded' by insults or slights (whether real or imagined)
- a lack of emotional depth and inability to feel or express sadness
- difficulty in sustaining personal relationships
- a tendency not to feel guilty but to blame others
- feelings of shame
- low self-esteem sometimes masked by bumptiousness and arrogance.

We may recognise in ourselves some of the signs and symptoms listed above, and we may have recognised them in others. Before we consider this further we might want to note that we may all manifest such signs and symptoms at one time or another, but that problems tend to arise only when they are manifested significantly and are prolonged and consistent.

Conviction and authority

There is evidence that conviction and authority, together, lead to narcissism. Some notion of conviction is important to Christians: it gives us the confidence to proclaim the gospel.

Authority is important too, whether that be the authority of the *Magisterium* in one part of the Lord's global vineyard or the authority of the Bible in another. If exponents of this theory are correct, the Church has the perfect culture in which narcissism can thrive! If we add to that issues of accountability and governance, we may conclude that not only is narcissism likely to be rife in the Church; it is also possibly beyond control.

It is ironic that the gospel we proclaim from conviction and with authority is a gospel of selfless love. Some authorities in the field of narcissism (as a personality disorder) assert that it is caused by fear rather than shame, yet the gospel of love we proclaim asserts that love casts out fear! We read in St John's First Letter, 'There is no fear in love, but perfect love casts out fear; for fear has to do with punishment, and whoever fears has not reached perfection in love' (1 John 4:18).

Narcissism in the Church ranges from a corporate narcissism which manifests itself in a universal arrogance (the Church may claim it has the monopoly on 'truth' in the face of other world religions), to congregational narcissism, where a congregation is so self-absorbed that it fails to be missional in any sense. Then there is individual narcissism, where people are so absorbed by an ideal (seemingly based in theological, biblical, historic or reasonable truth) that they do not listen to any counterview or opinion and then browbeat, bully or, by the use of emotional blackmail, persuade others to follow them. In this vast institutional Church, at congregational or individual level, we see the use of Scripture, historical precedent (including New Testament Church models), medieval imagery, theological constructs of God and derivative attributes of God as an image in the pool of our own obsession in order to justify our lifestyle, teaching or practice.

Conviction and truth

It might seem that I would condemn conviction. I do not! I am, however, sceptical about such conviction as engenders a view that one premise is absolutely right while condemning all premises that are different from it. Are we not all seekers after truth? Do we not all need the humility to begin the search for truth with the question on the lips of Pontius Pilate: 'What is truth?' (John 18:38a).

If there is conviction in the Church, then there are also deeply held differences of opinion regarding the conviction espoused by the Church. If there is authority, there is also fear of authority. In addition, there is confusion as to whose voice truly carries the authority of God. Fear in a congregation can stop its members from being open and honest about different views on matters of faith, doctrine, pastoral care, mission or anything else. Fear can prevent narcissistic leaders from being challenged. An anonymous survey of members of a congregation will reveal wide-ranging theological and ecclesiological views. Some views will never be aired, even among friends, for fear that such views may be counter to that being taught or to that which is purportedly held by the Church either locally or nationally. A congregation may include a significant number of people who hold similar views but whose views are contrary to the 'official' line taken by the Church. An example would be the difference between teaching and practice on contraception in the Roman Catholic Church. Another example would be the difference between the statement on human sexuality issued by the bishops of the Church of England and the opinions and practice of some same-sex couples, both clergy and lay.

Views being promoted by Church leaders are not easily challenged if there is little or no consultation on a particular matter. The situation is made even more difficult if people are afraid to share their own views with their leadership. This may lead to a situation where there is insufficient critical mass of declared counterviews to allow the official view to be successfully challenged.

Transition and narcissism

If we are truly on a journey of discovery of the truth we can expect the Church to change in response to its learning of truth. Even if the Church doesn't change significantly, the world has changed, and it is imperative that we are fit to engage with the world, to proclaim the kingdom in our own generation in ways that will ensure the message is heard. That, too, will require change in the way we do things, in the way we use our resources and in our attitudes and behaviour. Some authorities in the field of organisational change and industrial psychology assert that, whenever and wherever in an organisation there is change, uncertainty, lack of clarity of vision or unity of purpose, a climate is created in which narcissism can thrive. The work of Paul Babiak and Robert Hare, industrial psychologists and researchers, is particularly instructive here. They suggest that an organisation in transition can cause employees to feel uncertain. In a state of uncertainty they are vulnerable and easier prey to manipulation – something narcissists are very good at doing!

I mentioned earlier that the mythological character Narcissus died as a result of falling in love with his own reflection and that one version of his demise suggests he committed suicide. Whichever version of the death of Narcissus we may prefer, there is something in both versions on which we might usefully reflect as we consider, in this chapter, the relationship between ambition and self-absorption. In both versions it would be self-obsession and self-absorption that would be recorded as the cause of Narcissus' death.

For the purposes of this reflection, 'death' need not mean physical death, though there may be mortal consequences to self-absorption or drivenness. There may be, too, dire consequences for those who are victims of the self-centredness of others. Is not world poverty, hunger, starvation and death, to some extent, a consequence of individual, political and corporate narcissism? Those who are immediately subject to narcissists in positions of power and authority may be driven to despair or occupational or professional 'suicide' in order to escape the damaging effects of such subjugation. For these reasons, if for no other, we need to take seriously the phenomenon of narcissism in the Church.

Narcissism and vulnerability

Those working and researching in the field of human and social behaviour express a range of opinions as to the root cause of narcissism. Some might argue that it is based in low self-esteem. This might seem in contrast to any stereotypical assumption that narcissists are completely sure of themselves! Others suggest that shame is the root cause. Still others, such as the Christian American social observer and writer Brené Brown, writing about narcissism, distinguishes carefully between the yearning to believe that what we are doing matters and our tendency to confuse that with the drive to be extraordinary. We have already observed that we yearn to lean into God's ambition and hope to make a difference in the world. We are driven to proclaim a gospel message that is not ordinary but extraordinary. Here we should take care to distinguish making a difference from simply a desire to *be* different. The need to be different might present itself as the need to be famous, infamous or celebrated (remember Mark at St Stephen's?), all of which are characteristic of narcissism.

Vulnerability:
weakness or strength?

Taking Brown's observations to their logical outcome, we have a culture in the Church in which narcissism can thrive. Brown suggests that the fear of being vulnerable is at the heart of narcissism; that negative emotions played over and over in our lives feed our sense of vulnerability and that this, in turn, affects the way we live and work. In the context of the Church we can imagine how this premise relates to ministry and how it can affect those in leadership roles. Brown suggests that vulnerability is vital to living a healthy life. She declares:

> Vulnerability is the birthplace of love, belonging, joy, courage, empathy, and creativity. It is the source of hope, empathy, accountability, and authenticity. If we want greater clarity in our purpose or deeper and more meaningful spiritual lives, vulnerability is the path.[7]

Now we recognise the image and likeness of God in Jesus Christ! Now we recognise Love incarnate as a vulnerable baby and the vulnerability of the cross! As we relate such things to both God's love for us and our love for one another, we know the risk-taking and uncertainty in loving someone who might not love us back. There is no certainty in love but there is faith and trust. Certainty, not doubt, is the opposite to faith. Brown compares vulnerability with courage. We might find

---

[7]   B. Brown, *Daring Greatly: How the courage to be vulnerable transforms the way we live, love, parent and lead* (London: Penguin, 2012), p34

this a helpful thing to do. We might consider, for example, how we make ourselves vulnerable by asking for help, but how asking for help can take enormous courage.

Leadership in the Church brings with it greater scope to make a difference. What the Pope might say from the balcony of St Peter's Basilica in Rome is likely to be heard around the world. What a pastor might say from the pulpit on a wet Sunday evening in February might not be heard by many. This is not to suggest that the Pope is greater than the pastor (neither of them would believe that) but is rather about the scope of leadership. There is a connotation of power here, but does the Pope make himself any less vulnerable than the pastor? Pope Francis already has the reputation for a lifestyle which carries a degree of vulnerability. Both the Pope and the pastor show courage and strength in vulnerability.

By contrast, we may know leaders in the Church who are too fearful to speak out, even to express an opinion. Anecdotal evidence suggests that many clergy are at their most bold and courageous at two times in their ministry: at the beginning (when they are brave out of ignorance of the consequences) and in their last five years in ministry (when they believe they have nothing to lose). We may have come across leaders who are too 'buttoned up' to ask for help or to share their problems. Anecdotal evidence suggests that some in positions of leadership find it difficult to ask for help for fear of being thought of as ineffectual or weak. But how courageous it is to ask for help!

Brown links fear with shame which she suggests leads to disconnecting from other people. Such disconnection, she asserts, leads to a lack of empathy, and lack of empathy is a key symptom in Narcissistic Personality Disorder. Lack of empathy is not what one expects from Christians, let alone Church leaders! Brown uses the image of the Wizard of Oz who, having terrified the five central characters (I include Toto the dog in this), turns out to be a little old man with a microphone and a very powerful speaker system. Brown would seem to be suggesting that the Wizard is disconnected, that he is without empathy, and that is why he hides behind a projection of himself as powerful. Sadly, this scenario can be witnessed in many a church, chapel or cathedral on any Sunday of the year.

There is fear in congregations. There is the fear of challenging the narcissistic pastor who has become empathetically detached, perhaps through self-absorption or through burnout. A congregation may be afraid to challenge an overbearing leader in case they self-harm or behave in a way which causes some members to get distressed. There is the risk of deepening their own vulnerability. For many reasons it may seem impossible to say, 'No! Your behaviour is not acceptable to us.'

There is fear, too, that if seriously narcissistic behaviour were to be reported to the Church hierarchy the reporters would not be believed and that, even if they were, no action would be taken, leaving relations between leader and congregation even more difficult. Outside help may be needed, and before it is too late to prevent real harm being done. The Church hierarchy are sometimes praised for all they do in response to a crisis, but they are also sometimes criticised for doing little or nothing to prevent one. Unfortunately, some situations end not only in a lot of pain and suffering but also in a public scandal.

Congregational fear extends to fear of the world about them. There can be fear of people who are different. There can be fear of vagrants who wander into our churches and leave a bad odour behind. There is fear of organisations whose philosophy seems to be in conflict with their own. This, of course, is not the model Jesus gave us. It is one thing to assert that such and such a philosophy, teaching or lifestyle is 'right' but it is another to actively disdain, show disgust or to persecute those whose philosophy, teaching or lifestyle is different from our own.

The reader may recall our reflection on belonging first before addressing belief and behaviour. Again, we look to Jesus and his welcome of all as our model and inspiration.

Appropriate self-love

We are called to love God and our neighbour *as ourselves*. Appropriate 'self-love' is important. Being kind to ourselves, looking after ourselves is important. Could we perhaps hold that self-neglect in a martyrdom kind of a way is a form of narcissism? This might seem to be in contrast to the narcissistic self-grooming we identified earlier in this chapter, but this serves to illustrate the subtlety and complexity of the phenomenon. Brother Gerard's story might illustrate something of this:

Brother Gerard worked tirelessly for the sick and suffering until he made himself ill. The superior of his community took him to task. He reminded Gerard that although he had dedicated his life to the sick and suffering, he was a member of a community, the members of which had all taken the same vow, and that by wearing himself out he would not necessarily die but instead would be so crocked up that he would need a considerable amount of care from the community. Such care would take them away from the very sick and suffering people they had vowed to serve.

Workaholism can so easily disenfranchise others in a team or community who don't have the same capacity for work. The 'no one works harder than I do' mentality so often masks a fear of being accused of laziness or a need for sympathy or approval. Such feverish activity is more likely to be self-abuse than appropriate self-love, and is narcissistic. We turn again and again to what we understand love to be about. Self-neglect is the opposite to loving our neighbour as our self and, as such, is in direct disobedience of the Lord's summary of the Law.

We end this chapter, which featured the iconic mythological Narcissus falling in love with his own reflection in a pool of water, with a 'reflection' of a different kind.

Pause for reflection

For this reflection the reader might like to access (from the internet) a copy of a painting called *Washing*, by the German-born artist-priest Sieger Köder, which was inspired by the scene of Jesus washing the feet of his disciples at the Last Supper.[8] It features an embrace between Christ and one of his disciples, suggesting a fusion of love and empathy. The embrace is mutual and is not dominated either by Christ or by the disciple. Köder, with remarkably insightful detail, offers us in his painting the face of Christ reflected in the bowl of water he is using to wash his disciple's feet (John 13:3-15).

We seek and find the face of Christ as it is revealed in humble servanthood in a poignant 'pool' of water in this iconic image of humility. For Köder, Christ's face is central to the picture and is movingly reflected in the bowl of water. His actual face is buried in the deep and loving embrace with his disciple. Narcissistic as we are, we are still Christ's beloved disciples, and as such we embrace him in one another even as we are embraced. Narcissus sought and found his own reflection in a pool of water, fell in love with it and died. We see the image and likeness of Christ reflected in the waters of servanthood, and we live!

---

8   See, for example, http://www.course.soulspark.org.uk/Soul_Spark_Course/Session_4_
     files/4%20-%20Jesus%20washes%20Peter%27s%20feet.pdf (accessed 29 January 2015).

CHAPTER EIGHT

Final reflections . . .

. . . on being honest about ambition

Transparent ambition

It has been the experience of many contributors to this book that ambition in the Church is a matter of fact but that it is largely cloaked in euphemisms as if it is dirty or sinful. The reality is that some people are identified and steered through time-honoured and familiar pathways of ministerial experience in preparation for a more senior leadership role. Identifying and shepherding individuals towards higher office happens all the time, but it is a largely covert operation. From the time of the first apostles until now, we have seen some stunning leadership in the Church, but we have been wary of letting the populace in on the secret of their nurture. We have been quite good at not letting potentially great leaders in on the secret either! From time to time one hears that such and such a person 'is a good thing'. There may be general assent to that (whatever being a 'good thing' means), but little more is said until such and such a one appears in high office. What is the fear here?

It has been my experience, too, that secular organisations and enterprises are more likely to be open and honest about personal ambition than is the Church. In secular organisations people are openly recruited and selected for their potential to become key figures in leadership, and in some situations the absence of ambition renders people unsuitable for employment. Nurturing potential leaders requires dedication to their development, to their experience within an organisation. It is costly, but it is thought to be a good investment. Potential leaders may have to work in a range of departments carrying out a range of jobs, some of which might be quite boring or unattractive, but if the potential leader is to have credibility and effectiveness they will have to know how things work. Co-workers know, too, that someone is being 'groomed' for a leadership position and, in the more enlightened organisations, they are asked for their feedback on how the potential leader has performed while in their orbit. Such potential leaders are not always popular among the co-workers, but the process is open and honest and any significant faults are quickly fed back. The process can be beneficial to all concerned and can help to forward the aims of the organisation.

An open and honest recognition of healthy ambition in the Church would make it easier to identify unbalanced and pathologically narcissistic ambition.

Nurture of vocations within an open framework

God has been so generous in raising up, in every generation, women and men who have been inspirational and instrumental in bringing us back to first principles. We would lean more fully into God's graciousness if the vocations of future leaders were to be nurtured within a broader and more open frame of reference and support, allowing the laity as well as the clergy to recognise, support, nurture and celebrate the God-given potential of one in their midst. One wonders whether the other nine disciples knew that Jesus was preparing Peter, James and John for significant leadership roles in his Church. Would it have been obvious? His address to Peter as the rock on which he would build his Church is an example of this (Matthew 16:18). Did Jesus have to teach about generosity of spirit?

There is evidence that potential leaders are sought out and recognised even before they begin ministerial training. Where they are sent to train for the ministry betrays some consciousness of potential service. If a training establishment has a reputation for spawning a significant number of bishops, archdeacons and deans, it cannot be an accident. Not for nothing might a ministerial training establishment be labelled 'bishop school'! The statistics are not lost on the seminarians either, though they are expected to be circumspect in their reflections on what that augurs for them.

In the wider Church, lists are kept of potential leaders. Increasingly, posts are advertised and competition invited. There are many good quality clergy to choose from, and one hears of 'a strong field' of candidates for interview. One hears, too, of hands being laid on suddenly when a senior cleric feels Spirit-led to do so. Sometimes it is quite right to have done so! Networks of knowingness are the informal field for separating the sheep from the goats. Sometimes that works and sometimes it doesn't. Either way, the Holy Spirit gets the blame if things go wrong!

Stories abound of situations in which individuals have sailed close to the wind with regard to secular legislation. This has been occasioned because of suspicion of the secular human resources functionality and an 'above the law' arrogance, especially in a seriously narcissistic leader. There is danger here, and potential for serious harm both to individuals and to the reputation of the Church.

These observations and reflections are just a tiny contribution, a small pebble in the pool, not with an expectation of great ripples but simply of a stirring of consciousness to a phenomenon that is not upfront enough to allow wider support, nurture and celebration. Perhaps my question (rather than my assertion) is, 'Had it been so, might the infamous "glass ceiling" have been shattered years ago?' We acknowledge evidence of good practice, of openness and wide consultation. We recognise that some parts of the worldwide Church have been very good and robust in their selection processes, that they include rigorous psychological screening as well as wide consultation on the appropriateness of candidacy for ministry or high office.

We recognise, too, that self-serving ambition is not always evident in the early days of ministry and that, with its many subtypes and the skills of concealment inherent in it, those who are seriously narcissistically impaired are not easy to spot until it is too late. A second question therefore is, 'Were there more open consultation about selection and consultation about ministry and senior leadership appointments, would fewer seriously narcissistically impaired clergy filter through into the life of the Church?'

Honesty within a frame of reference

If a Church community or congregation were to regularly reference its activities to its declared understanding of God's ambition, it would have the opportunity to test its faithfulness to its corporate vocation and to review and appraise how well it is enabling individuals within that community to fulfil their personal vocation. There is so often a lack of clarity about corporate purpose.

We have already reflected on the diversity of opinion within a community about its theology of the kingdom. We have acknowledged that people can feel voiceless, feeling that they lack the eloquence or learning of their leaders. There is also a phenomenon of assumption. A community can go along for years assuming that its members are of a common mind.

Surely everyone thinks the same as I do! What becomes a matter for discussion is not the nature of the kingdom or our vocation in its regard but what to do about the church roof, the cutting of the churchyard grass or the proliferation of plastic flowers on the graves! Archdeacons, please hear me! I do appreciate that these concerns have their place. I simply suggest that if they assume a place above and beyond their importance in kingdom terms, they can become a convenient diversion from the awkwardness of talking together about God and God's ambition for the world.

. . . on being content

Brené Brown's research into narcissism through the lens of vulnerability led her to identify that there is a phenomenon common to most of us. It is the notion that we are never content. We are likely to consider that who we are, what we have in terms of personal attributes or gifts, and what we own is never enough to satisfy us.

Pause for reflection

The reader might like to reflect for a few moments on the subject of personal contentment. In what respects are you dissatisfied with who you are, what you have or how you are living? What might be the root cause of such dissatisfaction?

Being content with who we are, who we have become, with what we have achieved, rarely comes upon us in a mystical moment of revelation. It has to be thought through, sometimes agonisingly, and we should not expect the outcome of our reflection to be a constant consolation. It doesn't take much to send us spinning off into a whirlwind of self-doubt, disappointment (with others and with ourselves), anger, resentment and notions of 'if only . . .' We may need the help of another to return us to our sense of contentment – and better, to enable us to be deeply grateful for who we have become, and for what we are gifted, trained, educated and enabled to do for God. In this sense we can all benefit from a human reference point for exploring these things. It may be a spouse, a friend, a colleague, a spiritual director. For the character Shirley Valentine, it wasn't, initially, a human being with whom she shared these things. It was the kitchen wall!

The Conference Four on contentment

Do we get a sense that the Conference Four – Hugo, Christine, Ruth and Derek – are content, that they know themselves as satisfied?

We may ask if they have unmet aspirations. Perhaps they would reply, 'Yes and no,' or maybe it depends on which day you ask them! That might be more realistic. However, we might imagine that Hugo does not feel successful enough, that he believes that raising his profile will lead to greater opportunities not only to be more successful but also to be more acclaimed. He is likely to seek acclamation as evidence that he has done enough but he may simply get hooked on acclamation and never arrive at a place of peace and contentment.

Christine seems to know herself well and is content much of the time, but those who know her would know that she does not regard herself as good enough, brave enough or outspoken enough.

Ruth's pathway to ordination was hampered by voices around her saying she was not enough in the sense that she was born the wrong gender to ever serve God in the priesthood. Ruth is now secure enough in herself not to heed those voices, and she focuses her energies on all she has been given to do.

Her very sense of being legitimate and authentic renders her eligible for being and doing more as the Church broadens its vision of the scope for women's ministry.

Derek may surprise us. He appears to be content. He seems not to suffer from not being enough. Most of the time he does not, but he does suffer from self-doubt, from the feeling of not being good enough and smart enough. He wishes he had more power to change things, not so much in the Church but in areas such as global warming, carbon footprints and the conservation of wildlife. With regard to the Church, Derek was born and brought up in a clergy household, the son of a bishop. He has never been under any illusions about Church life or people. His father worked himself into an early grave because he never felt he had done enough. Derek has no intention of following his father in that respect. Derek has witnessed some wonderful ministry in his colleagues, and he has also witnessed some appalling behaviour among them. He is not bitter or cynical. He does not feel passed over for 'higher office' (his early home life put him off that idea!), but he knows plenty of clergy who are disappointed, who feel that their gifts, wisdom and experience are not valued, and for whom any chance of ending their life in peace and contentment is now (seemingly) lost. In his younger days Derek thought he might have liked to explore naval chaplaincy or even aspired to greater involvement in causes close to his heart, but not any more. If there is one mantra that plays in his occasional sighs it might be, 'If only I had been brave enough.'

. . . on being realistic

Earlier we made the connection between being real and being royal. Here we take that concept one step further and consider the need to be realistic in order to be 'royalistic'.

Having some idea of what our vocation is should also give us some idea of what it is not. It can be wonderfully liberating to be fairly confident that we know what we are not called to do, to know how we are not called to be. One hears this, for example, in a person who is wrestling with the matter of celibacy. There might be a sense of feeling obliged to live a celibate life, believing that it is necessary in order to offer the whole self in God's service. One hears of the pain of the struggle to sustain that way of life, and although some do sustain it and continue to believe it is God's will for them or the only way they can live out their Christian discipleship, others will come to an understanding of the appropriateness, for them, of a lifelong exclusive loving relationship with another. In such relationships they, along with celibate colleagues in the service of God, find they are still giving their 'all' to God, that having such a God-given human relationship takes nothing away and is not a compromise or a 'second best' to celibacy. The voyage of discovery of how best to live for God is signposted with being realistic, reasonable and honest with oneself.

Anything is possible?

We reflected earlier on the mantra, 'You can do anything you want to do, be anything you want to be.' How that sets us up for a fall! It is true that by God's grace we can do more than we might ever imagine, but we need to be able to see the difference between dream and fantasy. As we seek to discern God's will for us, we listen and look for guidance. It comes soaked in prayer and in self-knowledge. It comes in the voices of those who have a care for us: family, friends, soul friends, spiritual directors and those beyond the doors on which we knock as we test out possibilities.

For my own part, my life has turned out to be richer, fuller, more amazing and more fulfilling than I could ever have imagined or expected! God has been good to me, and I am grateful not only to him but also to all those through whom he has spoken. On the way I have noted the signposts of realism and have, with the help of so many, navigated a course that has allowed me to explore new and unexpected byways and to arrive in peace and contentment.

Consumed by zeal?

When we are 'on fire' with zeal for the kingdom of God and we are energised by the ministry afforded us, we can become so absorbed in it that we fail to see that people around us are not keeping up. We challenge them (if not terrify them!) or we disempower them because we overwhelm them. We can also neglect the very people God has sent to share our life, with resultant breakdown in family life.

Being realistic about our ministry is also about being realistic about what people can receive from us. As one priest put it to me, 'I am leaving that parish for pastures new because, although I am happy there, the people are now unlikely to receive anything else from me. It needs a different voice, a person with a different emphasis, different skills and gifts.' That priest moved on to do great things in another parish, and the parish left behind found new energy to support the new priest as they moved forward together.

By contrast, there are those who, having thrown themselves wholeheartedly into their ministry, have become burnt out. Going from being 'on fire' to burnout has cataclysmic consequences which may include the loss of family, friends and colleagues; chronic ill health or even death. Being realistic is also about being a good steward of ourselves, of keeping perspective. It is about saying 'yes' to God in the context of self-governance.

... on being governed

What springs to mind when we hear the word 'governance'? Rules and regulations? Close supervision? Constraint? The word 'governance' is based on a word which comes from the Latin via old French and means 'tiller' or the rudder of a boat. It is rather like the word 'rule', which comes from *regulare* and means 'handrail'. Guidance and gentle steerage is characteristic of good governance and lends itself well to the governance of the Church. We look for divine guidance through the Holy Spirit, and it is to be found in the Holy Scriptures, in the wise ones who shepherd the Church, and in all those God sends to walk with us in our Christian discipleship. Good governance is hallmarked by 'we' characteristics rather than 'I' characteristics, in collaboration rather than competition.

Freedom and responsibility: kingdom governance

Having zeal will always mean finding better methods of governance in the Church. It is always about freedom, which is the gift of God in balance with the responsibility that comes with the privilege of kingdom living. The theologian and Master of the Order of Preachers (Dominicans) Timothy Radcliffe makes the link between freedom and government. Referring to the constitutions of the Dominican order, most of which are concerned with government, he suggests that, surprisingly, government is not about division into those who govern and those who are governed. He refers to it as being more about sharing responsibility for all that we are called to be and to do. This implies cooperation, dialogue, debate and corporate decision-making. We might interpret Radcliffe's view as first knowing what one wants to achieve corporately before discussing and deciding on a plan of action and implementing it, the whole governmental process soaked in

Christ-centred missional purpose. Clear aims and objectives bring freedom from 'oughts', 'shoulds' and 'musts' that can so easily beset us because by agreeing what we are going to do in a place, a circumstance or a time frame, we are agreeing what we are *not* going to do.

Freedom is also about governance of ourselves as individuals and about the governance of the Church as a whole. Governance is not the same as constraint. Setting people free to proclaim the good news without fear or favour is hugely important. Ensuring that freedom comes with responsibility is equally important if bad behaviour is not going to thwart God's ambition. Making it real and keeping it real is hard work, not only for people in leadership but also for the whole people of God.

Shepherds and sheep

Jesus described himself as 'the good shepherd' (John 10:1-18). In that description he has given us an enduring model of ministry and leadership. At the heart of the 'good shepherd' model is a relationship of trust. The sheep trust the shepherd to lead them to pasture and to keep them safe from harm. The sheep know the voice of the shepherd; they recognise not only the shepherd's authority but also their gentle coaxing and encouragement. Those with any experience of sheep and shepherds might want to ask how enduring this metaphor is in contemporary life. Some people have never seen a sheep and don't even relate the lamb meat on their dinner plate to the woolly creature in the field!

My own experience of a shepherd was of a woman dedicated to the care of the flock, especially through the hard winter months and into the lambing season. However, by and large, the care and governance of the sheep was overseen not by the shepherd but by the farmer who employed the shepherd and was concerned about the 'yield' and 'market value' of a flock destined to be slaughtered by the end of spring.

The Church, too, has its shepherds with pastoral hearts, caring for the welfare of their 'flock', but there are, too, harsh realities about finance and affordability, fund-raising and contributions to meet the costs of ministry. The shepherds of the Church have to balance fiscal reality with pastoral care, and sometimes this seems out of balance. Some pastors claim that financial and other organisational matters take precedence in both decision making and the allocation of time available to address the pastoral needs of the 'flock'.

Beyond crisis management

We return briefly to a snapshot of shepherding. It is important to the shepherd that a sheep does not fall into a ditch because it can take a lot of effort to rescue the poor thing. A similar principle applies within the pastoral care of Christ's human flock. Here we understand that governance is more than rescue after the event, more than crisis management. To keep the sheep from falling into a ditch takes vigilance, firmness and careful handling. It does require some discipline on the part of both the shepherd and the sheep.

In terms of Christ's human flock we recognise the need for encouragement. 'I do appreciate my clergy,' cries a Church leader. Yes, but do you have the opportunity and a relationship with them which will allow such appreciation to build them up and to enable them to continue to work faithfully for the kingdom of God?

Having said that, it is acknowledged that some ministerial sheep are wilful and wayward and are apt to decline any help, support, nurture or training! Should that be allowed to continue unchecked?

Discipline and self discipline

If God disciplines those whom he loves (Hebrews 12:6), it is incumbent on the Church to discipline where necessary, otherwise the implication is that there is no love for such ones. There would have to be, of course, sufficiently robust accountability that those in the care of the shepherds of Christ's flock would have to heed necessary chastening. Is it easier to discipline after the event than to hold in check to prevent a catastrophe happening?

We should expect some accountability within the ministry of the Church. This need not be solely 'top down' – a concept that is uncomfortable for some ministers even though that is how it can feel! – but rather a matter of mutual accountability between leaders and followers, of mutually seeking out and bringing back the lost, of healing and reconciliation, of forgiveness and restitution. In this, whilst there is investment in leadership skills learning, there also needs to be learning and support for congregations and in particular for those through whom leaders lead. This would enable followers to identify and respond appropriately to any tensions and difficulties which arise and would help to prevent them from being manipulated or bullied by their leaders.

Learning from the past to shape the future

In order to consider how best the Church might, in the future, be steered more effectively into God's ambitions and in order for us all to live a more Christ-centred life, we might look to history for inspiration. Christians throughout the history of the Church have been disillusioned by the institution of the Church and the behaviour of its members whether lay, ordained or vowed religious. This has led both to reform and to persecution. From time to time, individuals or groups of people have set out to form communities which they believe will model kingdom living or which will more effectively foster Christocentric living. One such model was founded by Benedict of Nursia (c.480–c.550) who came from Umbria in Italy before settling in Monte Cassino in Southern Italy, where he lived with like-minded men who took seriously the call to seek God and to follow Christ and to live close to his precepts and teaching; to seek union with God in Christ. Benedict's twin sister, Scholastica, established a monastery for women nearby that was founded on similar principles.

Our knowledge of the life of Benedict comes mostly from the writings of St Gregory (540–604). Benedict's legacy to us is his 'Rule'. Benedict himself is not identified by any of his contemporaries, he left no other writings, and he does not refer to or identify himself in any way in the Rule. In this sense he models greatness in smallness. His Rule (as guideline and 'handrail') has had an immeasurably positive impact on the Church for 1500 years. At the time Benedict founded his communities and introduced the Rule there was a climate of uncertainty in the world. One can imagine what stability the Rule brought to daily life! This may be part of its appeal in our times. Benedict emphasises stability, continuity, balance, proportion, harmony and, above all, love.

Benedict's understanding of governance is based both in love and in listening in love. We are reminded that the word 'obedience' comes from the Latin *obedentia*, which is derived from two words, *ob* and *audiere* – 'being' and 'listening', or 'action from listening'. Benedict makes it clear in his Rule that listening in a community is very important.

We are to listen to one another even if a leader, appointed by the community, makes a final decision about a matter. Benedict also expressly teaches that the older members of the community should listen to the younger ones. He emphasises the value of taking counsel, of listening and of living with a disposition of listening in an environment of openness to hearing God's word and living by it. He ends the same chapter with reference to the Book of Sirach (32:24): 'Do everything with counsel and you will not be sorry afterward.'

Benedict promotes a life balanced in prayer, study, work and recreation. The leader, the Abbot (or Abbas [m] and Ammas [f]) is as Christ to the community. It is a model of servanthood in leadership. The leader is shepherd, healer and doctor. It is a good model of delegation and stewardship and is full of compassion and common sense. Benedict promotes a Christ-centred balance and stability by a *conversatio morum*: a life that bears the fruit of the Spirit (Galatians 5:22, 23). It has an appeal in reminding us, especially by the Rule's repeated scriptural references, to return to first principles. The Rule is essentially a guide to living a Christ-centred life and the more Christ-like we become the less self-centred we are. We need rules not so that they are a cage to constrain us but so that they are a climbing frame on which we can ascend.

... on the Conference Four

What is significant is that not one of the four of them – Hugo, Ruth, Christine or Derek – will enter into retirement significantly disappointed or at all bitter. This cannot be said for some in lay or ordained ministry. Even Hugo, as an inveterate risk-taker, would say, 'Well, I knew the risks. You win some; you lose some.' Hugo will reinvent himself in another environment and look for opportunities to live a full life.

Ruth will retire with the satisfaction that her generation of women clergy has made a contribution, has moved attitudes on while acknowledging that the Church remains prejudiced in so many ways and that there is still much to be done. She has nothing to gain of earthly treasures because all her riches have been poured out in the service of God, and she can prepare for retirement with a sense of deep joy and satisfaction when frustration and bitterness might have so easily been the case.

Eventually, Christine will lay aside her deanery and parish roles, citing the need to spend more time with grandchildren and a desire to pick up hobbies long neglected. Christine will continue to minister to her extended family and continue to be a good neighbour to all.

Derek will relax into retirement, content that he has done what he could. In the fullness of time he will retire to the east coast of England to pursue his ornithological interests and where he will 'help out' in remote rural parishes. At a retirement party, a banner would carry the words, 'All shall be well . . . it will all come right in the end,' adapted from a quotation from the writings of Julian of Norwich, the fourteenth-century mystic. Derek would be somewhat bemused until a parishioner would advise him that those words have recurred throughout Derek's ministry, have characterised his eternal optimism and have brought comfort and reassurance to his congregation in a range of challenging situations and personal pastoral encounters. Derek will be sadly missed by his flock.

Derek, Hugo, Christine and Ruth. When the time comes, each, in their departure from their current ministry, will leave a legacy. Each will have contributed to the building of the kingdom of God. Christian discipleship and ministry in some form or another continues way past retirement from ecclesiastical appointments. What might their obituaries yet say of them? Their 'end story' remains unwritten. What Derek, Christine, Ruth and Hugo will be has not yet been revealed (1 John 3:2).

Bibliography

Babiak, P., & R. D. Hare, *Snakes in Suits: When psychopaths go to work* (New York: Harper Collins, 2006).

Brown, B., *Daring Greatly: How the courage to be vulnerable transforms the way we live, love, parent and lead* (London: Penguin, 2012).

Church of England working party, 'Call to Order: Vocation and Ministry in the Church of England' (London: Church House, 1989).

De Waal, E., *Seeking God: The Way of St Benedict* (Beccles: The Canterbury Press, 1999).

Covey, S., *The Eighth Habit* (New York: Simon and Schuster, 2004).

Dewar, F., 2nd edn., *Called or Collared? An alternative approach to vocation* (London: SPCK, 2000).

Fry T. (ed.) and Benedict, *The Rule of St Benedict in English* (Minnesota: The Liturgical Press, 1981).

Ganss, G. E. (ed.), *Ignatius of Loyola: Spiritual Exercises and Selected Works* (New Jersey: Paulist Press, 1991).

Getty-Sullivan, M. A., *Parables of the Kingdom: Jesus and the use of the parables in the synoptic tradition* (Coalville Minnesota: Liturgical Press, 2007).

Moltmann, J., *The Church in the Power of the Spirit* (London: SCM, 1975).

Peck, M. S., *The Road Less Travelled* (London: Random House Group, 1978).

Pieper, J., *Death and Immortality* (Indiana: St Augustine's Press, 1968).

Radcliffe, T., *Sing a New Song: The Christian Vocation* (Dublin: Dominican Publications, 1999).

Stevens, R. P., *The Abolition of the Laity: Vocation, work and ministry in a biblical perspective* (Milton Keynes: Paternoster Press, 1999).

Williams, M., *The Velveteen Rabbit: Or how toys become real* (London: Egmont, 1922).

Wolters, C. (trans), *The Cloud of Unknowing* (London: Penguin, 1961).

Wright, T., *Surprised by Hope* (London: SPCK, 2007).